CONVERSATIONS WITH A
GNOME

M.E.Brinton

BALBOA.
PRESS
A DIVISION OF HAY HOUSE

Balboa Press books may be ordered through booksellers or by contacting:

Balboa Press
A Division of Hay House
1663 Liberty Drive
Bloomington, IN 47403
www.balboapress.com
1 (877) 407-4847

Print information available on the last page.

ISBN: 978-1-5043-4099-1 (sc)
ISBN: 978-1-5043-4100-4 (e)

Balboa Press rev. date: 10/27/2015

"If we shadows have offended,
Think but this, and all is mended,
That you have but slumbered here
While these visions did appear.
And this weak and idle theme,
No more yielding than a dream,
Gentles, do not reprehend:
...So, goodnight unto you all
Give me your hands, if we be friends,
And Robin shall restore amends."

Puck, Midsummer Night's Dream

Introduction

To make a family history story short, my grandmother, Nellie, was born in Cork and came with her family to this country. It didn't happen quite this simply, because they stopped off in South America for some years, but they eventually got to Philadelphia. My parents, siblings and I, and my aunt, all lived with her during my childhood. Her stories filled each day, and they live on...

In her house, the Little People had their favorite chairs. Whisking her hands in front of her as she entered a room, Nellie said, "Off with ye," and they rushed away. Making sure they had gone, minding their manners and not coming into her sitting room without her say so, she then told me to sit down on my red chair, and she would sit on her larger one. It was story time. Then, after the story, if she was not tired, she sang an Irish song. The Little People crowded in the door to listen.

They followed her to the garden and sat under the leaves of her rhubarb plants, keeping their eyes on her as she gardened. With my bucket and spade in hand, I trailed behind her, too, walking carefully between the lettuce rows.

In my childhood, the Little People, whom she also called the Little Folk, were everywhere, just out of sight, around corners, peering and inquisitive -- under beds, sitting on chairs, crouching down in cellar ways. The underground cellar ones were different and they were tiny. Mama called these Pixies. One of my younger brothers showed them to me one day. They were crouched in the nook of the cellar stairway. He asked if I could see them. At first, I said no, but then, after a while, I did see them. He had to first point them out to me, because they were in hiding, in the shadows. I think they liked my little brother enormously. He was elfin, with wispy yellow hair, and sparkling eyes.

The Little People I know are from all over the British Isles. The ones Nana saw were from Ireland and parts of England. The ones Mama spoke about were from Wales and Scotland. Most of Mama's family came from there. My father said the ones he saw as a child were in the woods of Pennsylvania.

In my childhood, I learned the Little Folk kept their boundaries. By day, the elves in the basement never came higher than the top cellar step. At night, in Mama's family, the custom was to leave a bowl of milk for these people, who included pixies, elves, sprites, fairies, gnomes.

Nellie had an awareness of something more. The house felt happy inside, comfortable, as if an invisible hand had made it a welcoming place. Not only her friends stopped by to chat, but also, animals and her unseen folk. The same feeling she had for an animal, making them happy, is the same she had for the Little People. You can call it all fantasy, but you will find life more complete and complex, to believe in something more than what is seen.

Nellie kept her house tidy for her Little People. She had 'everything in its place'. She said it was good luck to encourage the gnomes to stay as benevolent houseguests. She had beautiful objects in each room for them to look at: seashells, plants, paintings on the walls, books and toys for us in a cupboard underneath the green and pink Irish tea set.

At breakfast, she told the day's fortune with tealeaves. After she finished drinking tea, she took the leaves from the cup, placing them in her hand and stamped her fist on them. Each morning, sitting on a chair on top of Sears's catalogues and telephone books, I watched her.

"What do you wish to know?" she asked us.

"Tell us about the day," I begged her. "What will the visitors look like today? Who will they be?"

"Company is coming. One of them wears a long coat. The other one has on a hat. Oh, let me see, there is one with a flower print dress, that will be Auntie, maybe..."

Auntie Belle, my second cousin, whom we called her Auntie out of respect to her age, lived in a nearby town. Other aunts and uncles lived close to us, and always came by. Friends loved to visit; they came to see my grandmother.

When we asked her questions and watched her tell fortunes, there were the Little Folk listening underneath the table. I dropped them a piece of toast each morning. I thought they liked her current jam. The cat licked butter from the toast.

I started to write down the following conversations forty years after my grandmother died. She had many of her own talks with the Little People, as did my father. As far as I know, they never wrote them down.

These conversations take place in the remote north, a cold, forested area and they begin in early spring 1999, continuing through seven years. A gnome's New Year begins in Spring, so do these writings.

Spring 1999

Gnome sits on the porch steps, watching the fir trees blow and squirrels running up the branches. The wind shifts directions. He climbs up the railing and looks at winter's six feet of snow.

I'm outside, sitting in a chair on the porch and reading a newspaper. I am cautious not to disturb him by looking directly look at him. Gnomes often vanish if you look straight at them.

"Why don't you like it if people stare at you?" I asked him once. Other gnomes in the past had vanished when I looked right at them.

"It frightens me."

Once, when I studied dance, we learned that a soft gaze a dancer uses on stage, makes you aware of a peripheral area of vision.

He continued, "Look at me from the side of your eyes, which is where the other world begins. This other world is where we live. It is behind you, to the side of you, above you. The moment you stare into it, it vanishes. On the border of this world is where you will find me."

The problem is, you want to look straight at him: Gnome stands three feet tall. He wears a gold felt hat that resembles a crown. His green velvet coat makes him almost kingly. Leather pants, a brown shirt and suede boots complete his outfit. A white beard touches his knees. On each visit, he wears different clothes.

"Are you impatient?" I don't look at him, but continue reading the news.

"I'm waiting for the snow to go." He kicks at the snow bank. Gnomes like action, especially if you play music. Then they clap, and dance to flutes and fiddles. In winter, Gnome sits by the stove, sitting in a wooden chair with a red cushion that the cats love. He jumps on to the kitchen table.

The visits with Gnome started in this way: I came home from work, opened the kitchen door and saw two gnomes dancing on the table. When I looked at them, they vanished. I remembered my grandmother and her little People. I made a cup of tea and sat down. I waited for them to come back.

After that, the gnomes came each evening. They had tea, then stood on the table because it was higher than the floor, away from boots, shoes, cat food bowls. Watching them from a distance, I wondered how to make a conversation with them. Gradually, I learned to relax, and not to consider this imagination of mine totally crazy. I let my thoughts go out to them, and we began to speak together.

When they left, I thanked them for coming, saying, "I enjoyed your company." I never asked them to come back.

My day job is full of conversations with people. I work at a call center in rural Maine. Usually I do all the talking and feel I burden them with my cold calls -- phoning, intruding into their homes. When I come home, it's a pleasure to have conversations with a gnome.

Little Gnome does not speak. He communicates through movement, especially somersaults, jumps, and twirls. Almost two feet tall, and skinny, he is beginning to grow a beard. His face has scruffy whiskers. He is extremely shy and stays behind trees, or chairs. How do I know he is there? Leaves will suddenly blow up into the air. A low branch of a fruit tree will move. A cat will bat his paws at something behind a chair.

The Christmas tree stands on the porch, even though it is spring. Deep snow has hindered us taking it into the back woods behind our house.

Gnome, wearing a wool jacket and brown hat, is happy to watch spring from the porch. Grasping his knees, he screws up his face. His leather boots bend on the railing and shine with crease marks carefully oiled. I peer above the newspaper and start up a conversation – looking at him sideways.

"The snow sparkles. You are in a softer vision near me, as if you are part of a dream. Yet, you are real to me as much as the snow. Why don't I see you as vividly?"

He shifts his position as he looks at the fir trees. He says, "The essence of my life, when it connects to you, is partly in my own space, but, also, in your time. This moment is brief to you. It is long to me, because it is in another dimension."

"Can you see the snow?"

"Yes."

"Then why don't I see you as I see everything in front of me --I see you as a reflection."

"I am reflection. I am the snow. I am that which you know the snow to be, I am part of the crystals shining in it."

"Can you hear the fir trees?' Wind blows through pine needles. There are four tall ones in front of our house. Squirrels and crows nest there.

"I hear them. They speak a tree language," he says.

"Sometimes I think I can understand it, but my thoughts interfere with my listening."

"Then, let your thoughts have the wind blowing through them, just as the wind whistles in the firs. Clear your thoughts. Let the trees speak to you," he says.

I put down the paper, look out on the early spring and think about what he has said. When I look for him, to ask him another question, he has gone.

Snowshoes rest against a snow bank. I put them on to go over the snow to dump the food scraps in the compost bin. An eastern Mountain Lion and coyote, several skunks come for this nightly supper. Hauling the bucket to the back yard, I realize how bone tired you can get of beauty, of this white landscape.

Gnome and Little Gnome sit on a log. A small pile of wood remains of the six cords we got for winter. We are running out this year. How could we know this when we had our wood delivered last July?

I struggle for a conversation. What is there to talk about other than snow?

Gnome, observing the clear spring blue sky, points to the trees; fresh winds course through them.

"If you don't have anything to say, sit down," he says.

He watches Little Gnome twirling around as if the wind held him. Gnome taps his feet. I frown and touch my finger to the wrinkles on my forehead. Winter makes you think of serious things. In contrast, Gnome makes me laugh. As he wiggles to sit on the log, his round belly bounces underneath his red flannel shirt. Suspenders hold up his trousers.

Puddles appear. On either side of the path are five feet of snow. Gnome stands by the snow banks, observing the water. He wears fur boots.

"What do you see when you look at the sunlight reflected in the puddles?" He leans over, pointing to the movement on the water's surface. His short green cape flaps open. Underneath he has on a red flannel shirt and brown trousers.

He continues, "Light moves with the wind across the water."

Little Gnome, who sits in a corner, looks at the ice. He dons a wool jacket and brown pants, with a long multi colored woolen scarf around his neck, its ends tucked into his belt.

"Imagine being in this light, and you'd feel as you were skimming across the water," Gnome says.

"Like water skiing?"

"I'd like to water ski someday," His eyes twinkle.

The spring breeze again ripples the water's surface. Melting contrasts the frozen landscape. Closing my eyes, I picture a circle around me, full of light. I feel an Invisible World shining in this illumination. When I open my eyes,

Gnome is watching me. I am relieved he hasn't left. Little Gnome is trying to slide across the puddles.

"Light and water converge here in the water. These are powerful forces, transforming the cold to warmth," Gnome says.

A cloud blocks the sun's warmth. Light seems to leave the water's surface. I shiver and head for the door. We go inside to sit by the woodstove.

There are dishes on the kitchen counter, ball of yarns in baskets, bills spilling over the table. The cat sleeps under the table on a chair's red cushion. On the floor, shoes drift apart. I kick them aside – they belong out on the porch.

The phone rings. I stumble over a rug. It is my daughter in California. When I get off the telephone, my back tightens. I go over to where the stove is, because heat is comforting.

The gnome is beside me:

"How do you feel after this phone call?"

Outside, a squirrel jumps off the bird feeder. A nuthatch waits in the forsythia bush then flies for the sunflower seed mix. Our cat watches from the porch. I tap the window. I want the cat to stay away from the feeder. I rub the aching part in the small of my back.

Gnome says, "If you have pain, think on me. This is the simplest thing to say to you. To understand a situation, you have to go inside the person. Your pain comes from emotion. Love for your child, is love with difficulty – it is a space in which together you enter. The place is dark and not easy to walk there. Although you wish love to be happiness, it is hard work. You have to be in that place of the other where so much moves which is in darkness, because you are not that person."

Gnome wears a tweed coat of woven brown and a moss green beret. He sits on the dining room wooden bench, his red cheeks glowing. The cat sticks out her head from underneath the chair.

He says, "You are there together, but you have to change to be in there --listening, seeing where you can't visibly see, and feeling where you can't touch. When you can do this, it's like substance melts."

I look up to the tin ceiling of our dining room. My thoughts intertwine with the ancient flower designs, curve in perfect leaves.

Gnome waits for my thoughts. Finally, after dozens of flower patterns, leaves, tin curls, I look in front of me at the woodstove. Orange flames batter against the stove's window.

The gnomes vanish without me seeing them go. I wish I could have done this when my children were in their cradle and when I longed to disappear without them noticing. Instead, I rocked the cradle, as I sang and 'til they went in their boats 'cross the seas.

Mud season is here. Snow disappears, leaving dirt roads deep in slime. Ruts go a foot down on these roads, and I slide through them in my car. Following the mud trails, I know my car will make it. Other cars have been before me.

Gnome is with me as I head out of town on the muddy roads. I am going to play music for my friend, Mabel. We leave the tarmac road and start inching down the dirt one that goes up a hill to Mabel's house. The car slides and threatens to go into a ditch. This road is miles from any house and there is no one to extract me from the mud. The road has a Finnish sounding name. I call it just: Mountain Road. The next dirt road over the hill is nicknamed Gnome Road.

As I drive in the mud, conversation is slow. I do not chat with Gnome about any of the road names. I have to concentrate too hard.

Gnome is jumping on the seat. "Great," he exclaims about the mud.

"This is awful," I mumble.

I try to plan my songs. What music will I play for Mabel today? I swerve into a new rut. I decide on Gaelic work songs. She likes the harp to accompany the singing. Her farmhouse has a large room where the acoustics are good.

The farmhouse overlooks a mountain. From one window, you can see the sun set over the high hill. From the other side of the room, the sun rises. There are books written by her late husband on high shelves, children's wooden chairs on low bookcases, and an ancient family cradle full of blankets beneath the west window.

Mabel wants to learn to sing and I am teaching her.

With my car swerving, I cannot keep thinking on music and Mabel. I regret leaving the tarred road. On tar, you can let your thoughts ramble; in mud, you have to stop, be a Buddhist, be in the moment of the being behind the wheel, not cruising ahead into some ideas.

A glance from brown earth up, aiming the car out of billows because the sky is a still blue: I am ready to leave the car, and walk in the woods to Mabel's old farmhouse.

Gnome has his nose pressed against the window. I ask him to talk to me, maybe about mud? He shakes his head, continuing to look out. Maybe, he wants to arrive at her house in the car, not tramp after me through woods where there is a foot of snow left.

Mabel's large room has a fireplace and a long wooden table. An old oriental rug breaks up the open space. I start to play. Mabel finishes dishes, and comes to the long table. A black lab sleeps by the door.

Gnome creeps under the table. Mountains begin to cast shadows. A small gnome hides behind a chair. He might be Mabel's house gnome. He doesn't introduce himself.

Gaelic songs are calming. My hands are never nervous; they come alive on the strings. With Mabel listening, I feel a peaceful part of the music comes out. I can make people sleep and clouds darken. The time of the day disappears and seasons change. Notes go up and hang on the beams of the ceiling.

She shifts around the room, moving slowly. She pulls something out of a cupboard, shakes her head, stirs the soup, then goes to the cellar to load up the wood furnace. Sometimes I don't know she is gone downstairs; other times, she bangs a door then makes a clucking sound, as if annoyed at herself for the noise she makes.

Gnome stretches. "She is like a mother gnome," he says.

"Is this what gnome women look like?"

"Well, they are much smaller, but they have big auras."

People come into a room and you watch the space about twenty feet around them. They move without knowing what a presence they command.

Mabel's son in law comes into the room to make a sandwich. He stands in a corner, listening, and then he goes outside, maybe to the barn. Someday, he says, he is going to record my songs. He bought recording equipment to record local musicians. Mabel, watching him leave, stands at the window to watch the mountain lowering itself into earth. It is a sullen hulk, going into its sleep. Dark blue covers the forest.

"She is living underground," Gnome says.

"What do you mean?" I see how shadows spread on snowy fields, blackening woods. The inside of the house darkens. Mabel does not turn on lights tonight.

"She is searching for memories. She is tired of winter."

Some people think Mabel cannot get over her husband's passing a few years back. Weighted down by something, I also felt. I touch the strings again, one more song. When it is done, she doesn't say goodbye, only turns to the sink. Dishes clatter. Tap water shoots from the spigot. Music replaces words. She looks out the window. There is a grandchild's sled left in the field.

Gnome jumps in the car. We head down the mountain road to town. He holds on to the back of the seat.

"What is this road called?" he calls out about a road off in the distance.

"Mountain Road."

"What is that one called?" He points to the right as we stop at a small T- junction. To the right, the road winds up another hill.

"Gnome Road," I tell him this informal name. He smiles. "Children made that name. They see us. Will you take me on Gnome Road sometime?"

I have never seen gnomes on this road. Gnome Road has a moose bog by it. It is a place to see moose at dawn or dusk. People travel from everywhere to try to see moose in this bog. I met a person from Germany who said he had seen moose in this bog. What they don't know is that children have seen gnomes there, among the forest trees.

I tell him that sure, we can drive sometime on this road, after mud season finishes, however, Gnomes are in many forests here, right?

He is absorbed in looking out the car window.

"Let's think about what a road really is." He takes a moment before he asks me, "Well, what IS a road?" he says.

I answer, "We drive on roads from one place to another. We walk on roads."

He stands up behind me on the back seat. "The road isn't what you are driving on, going into the distance. You are not only sitting here present in time, but, also, you go forward in time, just as you go down this road, knowing it goes on, expecting that in the next fifteen minutes you will arrive at a point of destination."

Descending downhill on a muddy road is like skiing. On either side lie high snow banks with thick trees along them. I got into Mabel's house, so I guess there's a way of getting out, sliding down the mud.

"Never be bored by a road," he says.

Music runs in my head. I distance myself from this conversation now. I am learning words to another Gaelic song for Mabel.

Gnome continues, "Think about your place of destination. Place yourself into the future. You are sure of the bends in the road, the bridge over the stream. You take this for granted, because it is there. Try to move further than a mile. Picture what lies ahead in several miles."

I went to college after my children got through school, and afterwards I sometimes wondered why. You don't need a college degree to work in a call center in the rural backwoods. Listening to gnome reminds me now of how professors talk. I don't remember their conversations, of what they were saying, I only remember their hands writing on the wall's white boards.

Gnome waves his hands when he talks rapidly. He squints at the road, as we pass over the narrow bridge above a frozen brook. I think it must be very important what he is telling me, because he rarely speaks on a subject for very long.

"Time can go backward into the past. We remember what has happened through memories. To focus on time going into the future, take an external event from your day, such as driving down this road, and when you arrive home, take a moment to picture the event in backwards motion. This will help you enter hidden dimensions."

Holding on tightly to the wheel, I am perplexed that I cannot continue this conversation and talk about dimensions as he does. I can only experience them. I am letting the car inch through the ruts. Gnome has made the road into symbols of past and future. The past is where I had been at Mabel's farmhouse. Saying I'd be back; going out the door, into the future was a simple act, one that assumed I had trust for time giving me the moments ahead that I would enter.

"You can travel in dimensions this way. You review your day, from the end to the beginning of it. After doing this awhile, you may sense how you can put yourself forward into time, and then travel back to where you are now."

I snatch at the swerving steering wheel. Each activity with Gnome -- ordinary things-- like driving home today from Mabel's house, takes on a multi – layered aspect.

Yes, Mabel's husband died a few years ago and yes, I think, she may be still grieving him, but how are we to know, and she doesn't speak about it. For now, with me at least, playing music acts as balm to her, her eyes brighten ever so slightly when she listens. Mabel has a way of letting the night darken her room without turning on the lights, and she lets gloom enter in, because it is soothing. Music and shadows help perhaps heal her in a small way. We don't turn on electricity.

The road narrows. We go through a village. Even with snow patched in yards, the white banks hide the farmhouses. Fence posts stick out of ice piles. Gnome watches the water along the road.

One summer day recently, I had been riding a friend's Arabian horse along this same road, and Mabel sped past me in her car. The horse put back his ears. Yikes, I thought. Too late to wave to Mabel to warn her to give the horse room on the road.

"Mabel, slow down," I had muttered, not cursing for it was Mabel and I loved her no matter what she did, unconditional love you'd call it, I guess. But Mabel did not glance at the horse or me. She sailed with that car, over the bridge. The horse kept calm as I talked quietly, it's okay, okay.

Gnome watches a red squirrel run up the ash tree. It rests on a branch to look down. Above the trees, the sky is full of cirrus clouds. Standing by the window with him, I look at the sky; I being to float out there, imaginatively, of course; of a sudden, I am on a journey.

At first, there is a sensation of moving on. I visualize myself in a boat. If images come, they are separate from me, and I abstractly watch them. Gnome and I climb into a boat.

The abstraction becomes a painting, into which I enter: we see a harbor. Approaching it in the boat, we come to a city wharf.

"Do I go into it?"

"If you wish."

"How?"

"Focus on a point and go to it," he says.

"The city wharf?"

"You can be as specific as you want."

I step out of this picture. I am unsure of this journey. I need to come back to where I am sitting in my home by the window.

What would happen if I landed at the city wharf? How would I find my way? Was where I had gone, in my mind, the future, or was it the past? The city is like two places I already know. If I already know them, wouldn't I be in the past too easily? This was supposed to be a journey into the road ahead.

I don't encourage the gnome to talk, or ask questions. I get up from looking out the window and feed the woodstove. I remember how Mabel tended her stove, and how at her house there seemed always a space in which time lifted out of itself, as we looked at mountains darken.

Gnome enters my kitchen. The tea cupboard has a raisin jar beside the tea. I get out the tea bags, put them into mugs and place the raisins in another shelf, beside the oats, flour. Then, I walk to another part of the kitchen. The kettle whistles. I bring the mugs to it and pour out the boiling water. Black tea colors the heated liquid.

There is a flash of light beside me. It is in a place in the kitchen beside the cupboard where I have seen fairies – like a portal into another world in my kitchen -- but this time the flash brings a stranger, who stands in front of me. He is excitedly telling me that when I go to back to the mountains, everything will be different and I must prepare for this.

I make a list of what I must take. Such a thing as tea bags is an immediate simple thought, bordering on panic that everything is changing. The cupboards, floor, table, tea bags is my reality from this vision streaming in from somewhere, which could topple my life without any warning, or reason for it happening.

The person looks around, then, without any further words, he is gone, and I am left staring at the space in front of me where worn tiles cut rough patterns on the floor, black lines indent the faded linoleum. The teakettle whistles.

Small mountains are by Mabel's house. Further away are the steep ones.

Which ones did the stranger mean? Was it mountains in reality or was this a metaphor of some sort, where going to the mountains was a kind of journey. Mountains high in clear air, with a view below. You look down at your life, as if from the sky. The steep mountains have paths going straight up them. In winter, a chair lift takes you up ski slopes where you reach the top. Snow clouds block the view. Skiing down, you never go back up to avoid the fear, but up you go again, repeating the process of skiing down the slope: fear, speed, relief. It is a story of one's life – skiing.

French mountains, the Haute Alps, where I once stayed in my very early twenties, had life on top of them. People lived in villages on these high slopes. Shepherds tended sheep. Children played. Women with dark eyes, stared out of dark huts. My friends, who lived in these mountains, fixed up the huts and lived frugally. Sometimes I hiked to where the glaciers began and shouted to hear the echoes of my voice and I slept under the stars at night on high heather plateaus. Warm air blew up from the Mediterranean on those nights.

Gnome talks of inwardly visualizing places. I ponder the strangeness of non- ordinary imaginations. I can close my eyes and see each detail of memory, of newer experiences, like going with gnome in the boat, approaching the wharf and strange city.

Gnome is by the stove. Little Gnome stands near him. They look as if they know I will ask a question. They raise their eyebrows.

"I am in two places, the present with its difficulties for me, and the future that you wish me to go towards. How can I do this, when I cannot figure out much in my daily life?"

Gnome replies, "I have given you a lesson to learn about the past, present and future, by being with you on the road as you traveled. I need you to work with this for a while."

Bread bakes. I bake it chiefly for the family. The aromas should have brightened his spirits. I felt I had wrongly asked and waited for him to continue.

"The lesson I gave you was learning to be in substance, the moment, events -- things to be constantly worked with. You are normally, in your life not doing this. Were you to do this, the phone call with your daughter would not have upset you. The appearance of a stranger with a message for you would not startle you."

I glance at the loaves in the oven.

"This lesson is enough for now," he says

The oven clock goes off. I pull the bread out and put it on racks to cool. Gnome stretches. He finds a place on the rug, beside the stove to sleep. The cats curl around him.

The sock heel twists around. The stitches look uneven. I vow to give up knitting. I read the directions over again, and then place the sock into a basket. Was the vision preparing me for going to Mabel's? The mountain near her seems on a border of twilight. We'd let the dark come in.

The stove crackles. The cats go underneath it. Quietness brings the memory of my children who grew up here. Their leaving home made me learn to accept change. There is time to think about where I might like to travel again. Not in my imagination, but by packing my bag, taking sketchbooks, and going. To the Himalayas where the white peaks are like angels. To a northern Swedish forest in summer, with day never ending and the fir trees and moss growing over forest hillocks where the Little People dwell there.

Gnome shuffles into the kitchen. Cats look up from the rug. I stir the soup.

"I have a question," I say.

"Yes?"

"How can I be present in the place I am at? I want to be everywhere but here."

Gnome takes time to answer.

"Take a thought or a person that comes to you and sit still with the image or thought. Then, blend into it."

I close my eyes, and try to do this. "It feels like sandpaper."

He walks around the kitchen.

I ask, "If I think hard on the person it feels like dust disappearing. Have I destroyed something?"

"You have made a part of yourself come into the present moment."

"But, when the image becomes dust, is it gone?"

"No. By blending, being in it, you put it in its place."

Twilight deepens. Wind comes out of the forest, rattling the windows and drawing the air up the chimney, making the wood burn more quickly. I close up the stove to calm down the flame. Chimney fires happen when wind draws the fire too quickly up the chimney.

Gnome settles in a chair and Little Gnome creeps into the room to sit behind the stove. The sky is black beyond the window. I have the curtains open to see the stars. As I cook, I keep my eyes on the gnomes.

Gnome says, "You are losing energy if you are going out to these thoughts. Instead, picture them inside you, see what happens."

I close my eyes and this time I see a flame burning up pictures.

Gnome goes behind the stove. The Little Gnome sits in a corner.

Even though it is spring, snow falls again. What miracle will take away three feet of it?

Gnome tells me to become sleet, snow, gray skies. "Gradually, you'll understand you aren't that which you go into, you are only yourself," he says.

"It's the same," he continues, "when you die. Your spirit becomes the Universe. You cannot fear this process. You will go through it, and come out yourself. Your spirit goes to be with the spirits of time, space, stars, and loved ones."

I cast this part aside whenever he spoke about the life after we die. I wasn't ready for this thinking, yet little did I know during the process of our conversations that Mabel would soon pass on and my mother and father, too.

Gnome says, "When people die, they pass into the wide Universe, where everything which lived on earth is still vibrant, but invisible to earth. They are with the earth and you. When those you love pass over, you can connect to them as if you were blending into water and spring's new life.

"When a person dies, the body is gone, but the spirit remains. Think of those you love, who also wish to stay connected to you. They have passed into another landscape, which is Spirit Land.

"This is Eternal Being – fresh wind. You must let go, trusting, knowing their spirits live forever. There are many landscapes in Eternity. Each one requires a complete confidence that love will be there. Others known on earth will be there, too."

I have a small fear when he goes on tangents. "Okay, we pass into other spaces of time, other places, landscapes of visualizations that I have been doing with you, like in the boat – finding what I am seeking – I don't understand death too much, except it is grief, beyond bearing. That is what stops me from thinking about it very much – yet."

He replies, "I know."

"Explain?"

"In death, you pass into another sphere and cannot return, and grief is unbearable for those left to mourn. You pass into Spirit, which is in and with the universe and the earth, and is your own self and you are with those in what you call Heaven. It takes a while to get oriented. But you are still with the earth in spirit -- often."

I ask, "How does one walk the earth and be silent, gone in the body?"

"The Dead walk by the side of someone they know, and show them the forests. Calm them down from their thoughts."

He continues, "They help the earth, too. It needs peace to grow its plants, provide shelter for its animals, for its people, steady seasons and weather."

I move closer to the stove. He vanishes from the room. Gnome had said the dead want to help the living because they still love them. The world outside of my window is dark, and I am part of this darkness.

"Hey, come back," I call to Gnome as he looks around the corner. "One more question -- very important to ask."

"I need to know if you die, too."

"We can live a very long time. We are part of the ancient ones. We keep care for the earth, while you leave it. We are burdened with tasks, which are given us since time began -- to walk, rarely be seen through the forests, and meadows, mountains, deserts, and many more places. No, I cannot tell you about our deaths. That is not told to humans and only to us when we are ready to go."

Summer passes and it's winter again.

After work, I read beside the wood stove. Fire crackles and roars. Inside the stove is an inner landscape of color. Were this inner world to explode, a new planet could form, from its pure force of flames.

I read the NY Times. When you are tired of the forest land, picturing a city street helps calm restlessness. At this very hour, masses of people are walking down a street, traffic is racing – for a short moment, I want be in the crazy city, turn off on to Amsterdam Avenue to the Cathedral where a huge crystal from Arkansas is kept. I picture this crystal and above it, the large cathedral ceiling. I light a candle and set it in a small side chapel within this immense space and feel washed by a flow of inside to outer world. Then I step from the doors into the city, feeling jarred by its noise and people. I come back to a peace, of home.

The north returns: the fir trees, the frozen rivers, which are slowly unfreezing, the rural villages, all hours from the bustling city. What is the longing for a city when the forests are beautiful and quiet? What is the craving for seeing strangers' faces, hurried walkers on Broadway when people you see here are more genuine, interested in you if they pass you on a narrow sidewalk?

Gnome stands beside the stove. Far off in thoughts, where I was walking past stores on Broadway, I saw him close to me, sideways, wondering if he would ever be able to walk with me in a city. Perhaps, it would be harder for me. I would forget his presence and then have a hard time regaining it.

Gnome is wearing leather britches, a fern green shirt and brown wool hat. The woodland outfit blends into the trees. Gnome moves to another place. He looks at a painting on the wall. Then he sits down to talk.

"Today our conversation is not nature or people, but objects. Go inside the bureau in front of you. How do you get inside it?"

The bureau is an object I see a hundred times during a week, but never to stop and let it absorb my attention. Old and tall; it was given to me by my aunt. Below it on the floor is a worn oriental rug.

"Go into the rug," the gnome says. "Into the colors, the weaving, the worn threads showing, and a century of people walking over it, people unknown to you. Imagine whatever you can, but feel yourself in the rug."

"What is the point of this?" I ask.

"It is to be solid, feeling within material. It is a simple effort but you need to do it constantly. Then much else is peripheral to you and you will know how to be calm anywhere."

I concentrate on this and when I look up, Gnome is gone.

The next day at work, I sit at my computer, stare at the walls of my cubicle and down at the dull blue carpet. In the snack room, I put coins into the food machine, imagining into each detail of how these things are made. Turning from the machine, with my crackers, I look outside at the planted shrubs. Each year they grow higher. It is easier to put myself into a plant. A peaceful state of mind comes into me. I will myself to be present in the place I dislike most. When I get home, I do the same – I place myself into curtains, the old flooring, metal ceiling. It is going outward into objects as meditation.

In my dream streams thawed and birds called. My mother stood looking into her ancestral forest. She turned to me and asked, "What do you think the birds' songs are saying? Why are the birds always with us; what is their purpose? Then, in answer to her questions, in this same dream, a blue shining bird came to me and told me that they are messengers of thoughts. Songs carry thoughts. The bird said, "Tell your mother to send her thoughts to us and we will carry them to the people she loves on earth and in heaven."

Shortly after this dream, I got into my car to visit my mother, because I felt she was beginning to go through a change. Sometimes dreams are warnings. I drove six hours to the Berkshires. She came into the kitchen, leaning heavily on her cane, and smiled for joy to see me. I saw she was growing frailer. That night, as I talked to her by her bed, I remembered her as a young mother putting us children to sleep. How I long to care for her as she did for us. My brother care-gives for both my parents. He is single, no family of his own.

You have enough on your plate, I can hear her say this to me. Saying goodnight to her, after my arrival, she weakly smiled and raised her hand to mine.

I told her my dream. She listened. Her eyes lost focus. Was she remembering something? Bending over her, I heard her whisper, "Yes, the birds..." Her voice faded. She looked at the dark sky through the window.

As she stared vacantly, I thought about how I am hearing birds in a different way, letting my thoughts weave into their singing, feeling what it might be like to send my thoughts to them and let them travel with them into the sky.

Then mother told me that her mother had been coming to her from Spirit Land, and standing by her bed. She wore a beautiful dress, which my mother recognized. She was a young mother, bending over her child again. My mother said my grandmother looked on her with great love. My mother was startled because she felt her mother never loved her. My grandmother could be arrogant to people, seemingly caught up in society, wealth, material essence of life. I had loved her for something else -very simple things on my visits to her—her smiles at me, her elegant home, her beauty: watching her brush her long hair and stare into the mirror at herself, and at me with deep, dark brown eyes. They were eyes that knew people well, understood life but cautiously defined it in her terms. Whatever her behavior, I loved her, as much as I loved my Irish Nana, Nellie.

I wondered if my mother was thinking on her family in the starry night, longing to see them and entrusting the birds to take her messages to her loved ones.

It was hard to say goodbye -- I never knew when the last time would be. She held my eyes, as she does still now, begging me to come again. In great sadness, I drove away from her, waved goodbye, and traveled north.

She always had me call her when I arrived back home. Hearing her voice – oh, I'm so glad you made it!" I reflected on transitions, traveling, missing loved ones. What a strange thing is life. Leaving the most beloved people behind never feels right.

Gnome draws me out of my reverie. He talks about birds. "Birds are part of your soul. They sing the comings and goings of your life. Sit back in your chair when it is dusk. Tell them your wishes, and the events of the day. You will find that you will be lifted and moving on -- not out of your town -- but you will be moving in ideas."

Spring 2000

I hold a seed, feeling its round form. I reflect on how it contains hidden potential of growth. From this seed, a plant will grow. From what is invisible, immense life will rise. Holding this thought, I plant the seed in the ground. I picture the flower it will become. I cover it up.

"Look at the soil, grass, rocks, as you plant and take time to see the sky. Imagine how the garden will grow," Gnome says.

I pull stones out of the garden. "Do these stones want to be pulled out of the earth?"

"Some like to be pulled out. Others need to remain underground -- they hold earth secrets."

"Tell me about these rocks."

"Do you remember how we spoke about the future?"

The woods beyond my garden dip into a shallow ravine. I remember going into another landscape, where I was free to travel to the fantasy city of beautiful people, and where I had found a building with steps inside that I had to climb. I had grown fearful to go there. My fantasies are dreams in which nothing happens.

"You were enjoying learning to travel outside your body, in your imagination, but you stopped at a certain place and didn't go further."

I didn't tell him I was exhausted. I had to come back to my body.

He saw me frown.

"Let me explain. It is an image you seek for, and when you find it, go into it, let the pictures emerge and go with them. It feels like fantasy, it is-- it is your movement into the future. You will see how real it becomes, and then you'll see your life relates to your imagination -- it becomes nourished by your meditative travels."

A bird perches on the bird- bath, staring at us. I stand up to stretch and listen to Gnome:

"Who can say it is not the future you have moved into? You found yourself in a strange city. You thought it was a city you knew so you didn't explore it more. You approached it from the sea. The colors of the buildings were light blue and glassy rose. You didn't yet trust this magic."

He continues. "You need to close your eyes and go there again. Go back until you have found your journey. It will lead you to another place."

In fact I had gone back a second time and had not told him.

He seems to know. "You did go back another time. I was with you, only you did not know this. You got out of your boat, walked through the wharf area and picked a street to walk and then a door in a building to go into and then you went in and up the stairs, opened a second door, finding yourself in a room full of people sitting at wooden desks and they were busy reading papers. You looked more carefully, and said, "Oh, no, it is a publishing house!" You ran down the stairs, to the wharf, jumped into the boat and left!

"You went into this room, because it is part of you, yet you are running from it in your life. Don't you see how you found the place you needed to be? You needed to walk by each editor, smile and look for your manuscript and stand by it until you engage a person to talk to you about it. It is that simple. Go back again."

I get up from the row I had been planting.

The gnome waits. "Let's get back to the question you had about the stones. Pull one out of the earth. Look at the minerals in it. Imagine yourself in them."

The stones have mixtures of minerals. At first, they seem dirty and dull. On careful observation if I wash them off in the birdbath, I see sparkles in the rocks.

"How is it -- to be within these stones?" He looks at a stone.

"Look at the white one. Go into that one. It is a small part of the stone you hold, the other parts having broken off long ago. Focus on the part you hold. It is bright. When you gaze on it for long, you will be in a new place. Take time to imagine this. You can do it anytime when you are alone. Then, look at mica in the stone. It will also take you in imagination to somewhere else. Let yourself trust the pictures you receive. Remain in them, for as long as you can. After awhile, picture the hidden stones, which are deep inside the earth, and merge into their minerals, imagining them. You do not have to pull the stones out anymore. It is good to study the rocks and learn the different parts of them to gain an understanding of their ancient being and role in the earth -- how each one you hold is special."

I visualize rowing a boat. I find the tree, gaze beyond it, to the vanishing point and out to the sea. There, I am adrift, crossing the water to the magical city. I find the building, go through the door, climb the stairs and enter the door. Inside the room, there are many people at their desks, glancing through papers.

Going up to a woman at a desk, I find she is holding my manuscript.

"Hey, that's my story," I say.

"I know," she replies.

Piles of manuscripts are stacked on desks, and I realize she has many other people's stories there.

"These are all the stories of the world," she throws up her hands.

As she speaks, I notice there is a sudden silence in the room, as editors look up from sorting through stories on their desks to listen to us.

"You must tell me why you wish your story to be read," she continues, stashing some papers into a wastebasket.

I had written down in my notes of why I wished to write a story. I had imagined my audience, until I had my story boiled down to three sentences.

"I wrote this story because..." the words don't come.

I look out a window in that room, and remember walking down Broadway in early spring and seeing yellow daffodils for sale on every street corner. People rushed across streets between red and green lights. Cars screeched and a wind blew.

Those daffodils popped into my mind.

"I want to give a story like a flower to a city person."

Gnome pulls my sleeve.

"It's alright. You'll find the right words."

Frustration overwhelms me, and I turn from her, walk down the stairs, back to the wharf and the boat in which I row home.

Gnome and I walk through the wood where an old trail follows a stone wall. Small bush leaves unfold by the path. Wild flowers appear. These will grow and rarely be seen by anybody, because they are in a hidden part of the woods. Their beauty is inward. I sit beside these delicate whispers of spring to watch their loveliness.

I remember the journey I took to the city, and the editors' room, my fright and departure. Leaving quickly had left me questioning why I hadn't stayed and answered the person's question to me. I needed to ask Gnome if he knew.

"What happened to me there?"

"People are afraid of having their wishes come true," he says.

The wind takes hold of the top branches of the fir trees, moving them in a wave across the forest. I am on a log, listening to the gnome speak further.

"Wishes go out to the air and to the birds, and wait to find a place in the universe. You wish for someone to need your words. Wait, and visit your wishes, take your wishes to Broadway, and hand them to people. You can travel there in your boat."

Trout lilies grow. Ferns are at different stages of growth, depending on their species. Some curl in fiddlehead positions. Others open into a round crown. I have been collecting and drawing fern this spring, having concentrated on flowers last year. Eighty varieties of fern abound in the woods. Most difficult for me to find have been the maidenhair fern. Beautiful to draw, this fern, also, makes a good hair rinse.

Ferns remind me of my mother. She was in the forest beside the ferns, while my father hiked on with my brothers. She walked slowly with me. We listened to the stream rippling over the rocks, and felt the soft wind coming through the woodland valley; going on until it reached the river. Quietly she gazed on the plants, observing their detail carefully. Perhaps, she was inscribing each plant into her mind for a time when she could no longer be with them; when she could remember them and think on them.

When we go to the Spirit Land, when our time is ready, we shall remember the earth and the things we loved. Her favorite plants were ferns, wild flowers and the deep forest. As a child, when she and my father took us through the forest, I felt their deep love for nature entering me, connecting me to the land. She and my father seemed kindred souls. My mother was someone who in the essence of her being, was filled with radiance of inspiration. The plants seemed to give her peace.

Each morning's hike in the forest, my father showed me the fresh animal tracks and pathways; never disturb an animal trail, he said. He taught me to love trees and to count stars at night, and to make a wish as we watched them shooting through the sky from the cabin porch.

I get up from these memories, leave the woods, and return to the garden.

Gnome accompanies me to the third floor, where mice scratch and squirrels run inside the roof, the cats huddle in corners trying to catch these creatures. Sometimes a squirrel will find a way to get into a room. A mouse darts across the rug, and hides under the rope bed.

Inside the high windows, between the glass panes and screening, wasps build nests. I catch the wasps without harming them, by placing a glass jar over them, opening the windows and putting them out on a roof ledge.

Looking out over the town from up here, I reflect on my boat journeys, which is in my imagination – all these conversations are in my imagination, too, remember -- to the editor's room. I had found it easy to visit this place at any time -- in a split second I could be back there. One time I was staring at the desk piled with papers, the gnome peered over the desktop, and the editor looked up, seeing me.

"It is simple. Don't complicate anything. Take just a few things along. Apply this to your work. Say what it is you wish, and the answer will come. Do not rework to find the hidden element of a story. That is not the way," she said.

I did not have to worry about the words she was reading. She was actually beginning to read my story. Leaving the room in happiness, I went back home in my boat with Gnome. I thought I saw Little Gnome, hiding under a boat seat. I was back in the garden.

"What do I do next?" I turn to Gnome.

"Take a walk."

We start on the forest path, with cats following. My walks in the woods are like this, they include my cats and the gnomes – creatures alike in lone wanderings. Glad for aloneness, I am musing about how to explain walks with Gnomes. Someone once said one musn't worry what the world thinks -- the artist creates new worlds. I decide not to explain anything rationally. What I see, even if in my mind, is a creation of words.

We don't converse. Instead, I watch the path, keep from tripping on tree roots. We pause on a footbridge to watch water boatmen, insects which skim the water surface of the stream, and hide under rocks. They dash out to grab a fallen twig, thinking it another bug. The gnomes giggle. I wonder what lesson there is in observing this, but the Gnome prefers to be still.

When I am home again, I climb the attic stairs and flop down on the old rope bed of my great aunt's. I pull a cover over me. I awake to the sun coming in from the window. Gazing out of it, I follow a distant object, a tree branch, concentrating on departing from my place of sitting, finding myself within the boat, drifting over the sea to this city, and building in which I felt slightly less fearful. Nothing new happens, I take the journey, finding it enjoyable now, and even the color of the sea is uplifting –blue, gentle waters, rocking, lulling me to comfort, acceptance of just being there.

Gnome and I sit on stones. Woods smell of moss. Streams rush with high waters, and birds dart into bushes. I am taking my mind from things, letting peace come into me and flow back out.

I'd been hiking with Gnome, Little Gnome and a cat, and a sudden crash erupted, like someone stepping on a rotten log. We watched in the direction of the sound for what seems a long time, but might have only been ten minutes. If it were a cougar, bear, porcupine, moose one of us would be the first to move. They say in the woods you are never far from a bear or a mountain lion. However, nothing stirred. If it were another person in the woods, I would move swiftly to hide, blending into the thick growth of briar bushes and gnarled branches, which had fallen along the swamp.

Now, with Gnome, I am looking for ferns and flowers to draw. Nearby is a place of wild irises, the leaves are only seven inches high, with no blossoms yet. The forest is quiet again. A falling branch, forgotten. The cat settles on a stone.

We inch through brush, seeing if we find more ferns between branches and logs. There are supposed to be eighty- seven varieties in these woods. Like a moose, we go through narrow spaces. Gnome interrupts my thoughts:

"Walk this way in your day. Move carefully through situations. Where the landscape becomes your soul, your house becomes your thoughts; the extent to which you travel in these thoughts is your future. Head out to sea. Maybe you will sail past the city and the room with the desks will be gone. Then change will have happened in your life."

We tramp in the forest, practicing being moose, slipping through spaces, then we head home. Gnome and Little Gnome vanish.

I had to take vacation time from work . I'd used up my sick leave. Colds, sinus infections, migraines, or constant bleeding assailed me. Sometimes I blamed it on the air quality, but the managers said the air system was working fine. Other times, I blamed the chemicals in the rugs, or artificial walls of the cubicles in which we sat. Who knows?

I bled all the time. Wearing sanitary napkins as well as tampons, and going to the bathroom every ten minutes to check I hadn't leaked on to my clothes and seat, and managers watching their watches to see how long I took to do this; I was living in deep pits.

Added to this, the gnomes left me. I went to an acupuncturist, but my insurance didn't pay for this so I stopped, and then I had operations, which helped awhile. My mind began to clear and one of the first things I heard when I looked out my window in the morning was a bird calling, and I imagined it passing over the lawn, although I could not see it from my bed. I imagined myself on the current of air that it stirred up over the lawn, and I immediately felt like rising up out of bed. The mind has great power. I told myself, and I can get well again.

One day, Gnome suddenly jumped on my bed. He had returned. So, I asked him, "How is it I feel that bird helped me and healed a piece of earth it flew over?"

"It flew in a motion of energy, which was like wind and went over the ground beneath it. You can always access the healing the birds give to you, only you have to be in rest and a place of stillness to receive it," Gnome answered.

Invisible currents of motion set up when the birds fly. Wind is a powerful force for us. Each wind is the earth's breath and when it touches us, we receive freshness of life. We, even unconsciously, receive grace and it constantly enters our lives.

From my room, I hear wind brushing branches against the walls. Wind movement produces circulation over the earth. These are healing forces. Although I can't see Gnome because my energy is low, I can hear him. He shuffles around. Curtains stir by his presence.

Early summer 2000

Winter was long this year and spring, very short. Now, trees leaves are fully open, spreading shadows on the lawn. The delicate green color, my favorite, is so soon gone, and green is heavier now in hue and foliage. Spring with its light, fairy nature and turned into sullen summer, burdened with weight. Trees bow their branches.

Gnome, roaming woods and meadows, stays hidden. Is he avoiding meeting me? A human being can be frightening, if a gnome doesn't wish to be social. Sometimes, I think I see him and Little Gnome.

I might be thinking a thought, walking or gardening or out under a tree reading, and suddenly sound, and energy, and a friendly warmth enters my heart, which I recognize as the gnomes, somewhere with me, yet distant, caught up in the summer world.

Gnome says, "The earth is constantly being healed, because it is continually harmed. Birds, bees, butterflies, which fly over the earth help to heal it. Every movement of wind in the trees heals it. There are winds which are not of healing, where the emotions of people -- anger, passion, despair are captured in them, and then we have to ponder these angry winds and how to heal them," he says.

Looking into the sky, relaxing into summer, I watch the clouds above me. I have this telemarketing job, because it is the only job hiring and it gives health insurance benefits for my family. My husband has lost his job. But isn't it, I tell myself, ironic to work for a job that gives great health insurance, but also makes me sick?

Gnome says, "Live into each day and see some part of its beauty which is much more than any sadness. Yet, there is sadness. You are feeling it, but it is not yours. It is of the bleeding of hearts suffering in the world. You cannot heal anything that does not come to you for healing -- you can pray for the healing, leaving the Universe, the angels to heal it over time. It is not an easy thing to leave a situation alone, and to pray for it when you are distant from it. The bleeding heart, the bleeding soul, is part of the bleeding world. Be in your sorrow, open to your sorrow, accept each day as it comes."

My daughter has been in the hospital out west. I call her but she has not much energy to talk. I realize I cannot change the situation, make her health improve. I sense she wants distance.

Where Gnome and I rest, branches have bent down to the ground from rain. Summer rain can be drenching, but after it, the forests fill with mist. At the top of the firs, fog lifts into the air, and clouds drop to catch them. The forest and sky blend.

Gnome speaks, "You cannot change someone else because you wish it. Changes take many life situations and circumstances. There is only one change possible-- that is within you. It is hard to change yourself and to be in your family setting when you are changing. This is the hardest life situation because you wish family members to acknowledge you as changed. The act of awareness is to see when someone has grown and moved into a space apart and to know it, let them live in this new place. Bow to them in respect of their enormous step of self departure."

I think of my boat as my own departure.

Raspberries ripen. Fruit trees cast shadows over the yard. Bushes and ferns blow from a soft wind, and movement seems to unite this summer world.

Gnome says, "Relationships weave together. The trees need the flowers, which need the shadows, which fall on berries and grasses. Even the butterfly breathes as it passes through."

The forest has a small waterfall, which crashes on rocks. This paradise is where in some hidden world, winter never exists. Summer is eternal. Here, there is safety, refreshment.

Gnome positions himself on a rock. His green jacket hangs loosely, and he takes off his hat.

"Changes will take you in their grip with hard times, then let you go, allowing you freedom to decide what to do. Work with what is in one day, knowing that someday, when it is your time, you will be leaving earth -- that is the way of life."

Perhaps, he wants to ramble on further in the woods and go on the paths over the footbridges. He seems to like where he sits. I get up to wander along the stream.

Both gnomes follow me. If I forget to mention both of them, it is because I have come to take the young gnome's presence for granted. Sitting in these woods, Gnome and Little Gnome watch me. I am beneath a fir tree, looking at a rock, which I call the angry rock. It is angry because in winter, it hates the hard ice pressed against it, and in early spring, rushing waters swarm by it.

In this late summer, the weather is turning dry; part of the stream stops flowing. It is running underground and the angry rock seems different. It curls in on itself. As I look at the other rock beside it, this rock is listening to me. In it is a wise Being who understood anger. This Being, if taken out of the rock, would look like a wrinkled, old man, with a sparkle in his eye. He is trapped inside this rock, and someday, he will get out.

The gnomes watch my interaction with the rocks. Gnome and Little Gnome wear brown jackets and green shorts, which blend into the tree trunks and forest fauna. The green shorts are the color of ferns and moss. Their brown boots are the color of mud.

"Is this the right rock to speak to? I am angry so shall I speak to the angry rock, or the wise one?"

Gnome replies, "You decide."

I tell the wise rock about my job. My managers want you to be so professional but do not act it themselves. I had been angry with two managers because of this and had stepped out of my place to object to the head manager about them, and how it made me lose my own power and I that is why I haven't any energy.

The wise rock, covered with moss and lichen over its granite surface, looks at me with understanding. It is what I needed -- a rock to listen to me.

Gnome says, "You will find that rocks come alive. Find one you like, and talk to it silently, and it will converse with you in visual imagery."

I continue to return to this rock. The rock is in the deep forest where no one hears me. Daily, I let out my frustrations over my work, and how I cannot leave this job I loathe. No one likes telemarketers calling them. They do like it if I make transactions for them to save money, but that is rare that we can do this kind of bank account work. Once in awhile we shift to another division of the bank company that deals with their own customers. The stone gives me no answer when I complain over the job. Leave the job, my friends tell me. However, I have to earn for the family. What I like about the wise rock is its listening, and maybe that is all I need. I am in the middle of the woods and no one, besides the gnome, will see me talking to stones.

Silence in woods, these days. Birds perch in trees near the pond. In the heat, dead leaves from last autumn resurface on the forest floor and crunch under foot.

The air crackles as a dry wind blows through bushes. A match, a campfire – could ignite a forest fire. I feel as if calamity could happen, like an enormous lightening storm moving in.

On my walks, I note changes in the rocks. I ask the gnome why the angry rock had been uncommunicative with me.

Gnome says, "Well, it is easy to think about. When the seasons change, back in winter, ice is heavy on it, and waters rage past the rock. Didn't it, back then, tell you that it is angry at this intrusion on its territory?"

I affirm that yes, it is so.

He replies, "There is no peace for the rock. When there are days of heavy rains, or melting of snow in the spring, it has to endure this state of affairs where the stream overflows it banks, and creates a whole new stream, which rushes around the rock, constantly disturbing it."

I look more at the rock on walks and observe it doesn't seem to speak anymore.

Gnome tilts his head. He looks at little gnome and shakes his head.

"Simply observe the angry rock."

"Why?"

"Look again."

The rock seems soft as a sponge.

"The anger did this?" I ask gnome.

"You see, the rock lost its anger, because you turned to the other one, the wise rock. You can find wisdom turning from anger, or even going through anger, but staying in it will make you lose part of your form. The wise rock sits beside the angry rock. Only the angry rock does not wish to learn its lesson and go from anger to becoming wise. It is upset because now the water is not flowing by it and since it is always angry at the water, there is nothing to be angry about, so it cannot find its existence apart from the anger."

I lean on a white birch, close to the rocks. The bark is peeling in sheets of bark. The gnomes are at my side. Around me is the pathway of the former stream. At the edge of the woods in the near distance is an old stone-wall, and remains of a clearing where once sheep and cattle had grazed.

Gnome speaks, "Before the stream was here -- ages ago-- the angry rock was surrounded by gentle woods. When the stream broke through and made this channel, it was annoyed and bitter to have its existence change, but instead of accepting the change, it found anger and has become this anger. It has lost its ancient sense of time, long before your humankind grew on earth."

Rocks, contrary to trees and plants, last a long time. Geologists walk these woods and find traces of glaciers, write up their research work, yet never know what it is like to be a rock.

Gnome continues, "The angry rock will be at peace in some future time, only it will then have accepted it is only a small rock and the peace around it was part of it, but it did not see that. Anger is a strong force and we think we are powerful when we are angry, but we are not."

This conversation brought me back to my workplace trouble, my own anger. The gnome seemed to know about it. It would still be sometime before I felt I was ready to invite the gnome to come to work with me.

In the heat, rocks are soothing to be next to because of their cold surface.

Gnome says, "Your boss is curious about you. He watches to see your anger will make you fail or succeed."

Fail or succeed? I had not given that any consideration, because I would only consider this a day job, which I have to keep.

"You will succeed if you learn the power from success is your own inner fire of ego. Be strong, be wise, let the anger go. Peace is your strength."

My throat is sore. It is from speaking to many people over the telephone each day at work. In between work, at home, I am silent. I go to work, talk on the phone, say nothing to my co- workers, and return home.

The wise rock is quiet; the angry rock frowns.

Little Gnome touches their rough surface. He looks up.

Big Gnome says, "We must go."

I see them tramp on through the woods, as I head home.

Gnomes roam the forest, seeming like cats that keep their eyes on humans and stay in their own territory. When I want to have conversations with them, it doesn't always happen.

For instance, I can have a week when I am upset by my job and unable to communicate with them. In such times, there is nothing to do but wait, and work hard at my frustration, think about finding a new job, or improving my attitude towards the present one.

When I think they have given up with me, never to converse again with me – they come back again.

I am on my way to an art lecture. They sit on the car seat with me.

"What are you doing coming with me?"

"We want to see the cat lady," Gnome says.

"You must be mistaken. I am going to a place where there are famous artists, not ladies with cats."

"You will see," Gnome replies.

Where we go, the art school lecture is in a barn. People sit on wood benches. Once the walls had been rough clapboard slabs, but now they are sheet rocked and painted. A few rafters have been replaced. The lecture area has a make shift stage with white wall behind it. One side of the barn's interior has large murals, and over the years, a few of these remain, while new ones get painted by students each year, on top of the old. Some summers had political themes, others were sex and violence, spiritual and demonic themes -- it was there on the barn walls.

This year, murals are on three sides of the barn. Their size is five feet by five. The themes are landscapes and people: millers, farmers in fields, union men standing outside factories, naked people -- all saying to me that time is not eternal; the body is heavy. The conditions of life drag us down into monotonous images. One mural had fish dangling from lines like symbols. Seek and you find and catch fish.

I wondered why I have come to the art lecture on this Friday evening. The previous summer Allen Ginsberg had been there, reading poetry, tapping stones, and getting us singing a William Blake poem. The name Ginsberg had drawn many people.

Students sit up straight on the benches. The guest artist appears on stage, opening her show by explaining the stage is not her place of energy. Surrounded by people on all sides of her is where she best feels comfortable, rather than on a stage. A circle is her space, and a circle can be painful, she says. People can come too close, or they can be too distant in a circle.

The gnomes sit with me. I've made sure there is room for them on the crowded bench. One aristocratic city looking person looks at me strangely, when I explain two places are taken, when he can see they aren't. (He thinks). The gnomes watch the artist lecturer, a woman who is pretty in her middle age. She moves as a dancer. She looks like she had starved most of her life to have a dancer's body. Although young looking in her limbs, her face is heavily rouged and it shows the strain her body has gone through by staying very thin. It is beginning to wither.

She shows videos of her paintings and dance performances, where she had combined her love of her body as form with colorful, visual images. In what would be questionable for a performance in my town, a half an hour away, was acceptable here. Read on to understand why.

In the video came other female dancers with her, who all pulled SCROLLS out of their VAGINAS. The artist explains that the symbols on the scrolls represented the body's INTERIOR wisdom.

Gnome whispers, "This is ANCIENT wisdom."

The dancers on the video performed with paintbrushes. As they danced, they painted each other's bodies. They picked up fish and chicken carcasses and draped them around each other's heads and necks.

The gnomes are spellbound. Old gnome squints.

"What do you think?" he asks.

I whisper so that the man on the side of him does not look at me.

"Gnome, I am rather conservative in taste. I prefer her landscape paintings to this. Her paintings expressed depth and form. The paintings are good. The dead fish and chickens and symbolic vagina scrolls in the film are grotesque."

"Do you also look at her?" he asks

"Yes."

"And?"

"She's unusual, kind of elegant. She walks with ease, as a dancer. She is conscious of how she lifts objects, and even beautifully hands the microphone to people in the audience to ask her questions -- she has grace. She walks in air, not on ground."

"What else do you see?"

I ask, "What do you mean?"

"Look at the space around her head."

I tell him, "I see her aura is yellow, laced with white. About two feet above her head violet light rays out. Her vibration is soft, but powerful."

"That's accurate," the gnome says and resumes listening to her speech.

She is talking about how she gets inspiration from ideas and moves in and out of them. She uses her dreams for art themes. Then, CATS inspire her.

So- here was the reason for the gnomes to come here.

The cat, she is saying, is a PARANORMAL guide to her. She has many photographs of her cats in a gallery in San Francisco. The cats have mystical qualities, associated with the feminine aspect of a person. Our society, she said, has made women into sex symbols. However, the real symbol of the feminine is Mystery.

The cat in Egypt gave the breath of life to chosen youths who were destined to become visionaries. The cats breathed into the mouths of these young children. This was a special breath, allowed only to a few youth to experience. The cat stayed with the child over many years.

She shows films of one of her cats with whom she felt mystically connected. This one cat is beloved over all her cats. It is in many photographs. It puts its nose to her nose, breathing into her.

Gnome is transfixed. He sits without swinging his legs on the bench – back and forth.

"We'd like to meet this woman."

I lean over towards him:

"Why don't you?"

She says how Art is vision and dream. Not career, strategy and curators, but she told the students they would have to learn to do all the business aspects of art-- what she had to do-- to become artists of our time -- learn to write grants and fellowships, to take rejection of one's art until success comes, when a museum buys your art.

"Remember -- art is vision," she says.

The gnomes swing their legs so fast they are about to rock off the bench.

"What is in the white laced light around her?"

I closely look and reply to Gnome.

"Give me a moment."

Sometimes I see auras- like halos- and some people because I get migraines say it's because I have migraines, but I say, who knows why we see what we see. I have never been able to intervene in anyone's aura and change its color. There are colors around every person yet not every aura shows itself to me. I take that I'm not meant to see it, and it is okay that way. I have to turn off like a switch some of these things I see because it gets to be too much, overwhelming, but Gnome had asked me to see this person's halo -- An aura is simply an extension of a person. Auras of artists – musicians, dancers, painters -- constantly change colors.

I answer, "The white light is delicate, like a web, meaning she is very sensitive, but she has patience. She waits for insights. She does not run after things. This waiting gives her a soft radiance."

In this lecture barn, full of young art students on their way to fame someday – for no one is excepted here who isn't fabulously talented, they say-- she is now talking about how many affairs in her past she'd had with men, how exhausting to her creative energies these had been. I wondered if men still sought her. It came to me that she did not have that happening anymore.

I tell this to Gnome. "She may be alone and having to deal with loneliness."

He looks down at old wooden barn floorboards.

She is saying her most beloved cat died. She has tears in her eyes. Her tears make people wipe their own eyes. She traveled everywhere with this cat.

The little gnome looks startled when she finishes talking about that subject.

Gnome says as he looks up, "She is alone now. If only she could find us, the gnomes. We'd keep her company. She could put out a bowl of milk each night for us."

I look sideways at him. She has smote him, if you can say that about a gnome.

Gnome goes up and stands in front of her, but she looks straight through him. He puts his head down and walks away, out of the barn.

On our ride home from the summer art school, I ask Gnome about love. I am curious if gnomes experience love.

"Do gnomes love the same way as we?"

He retorts, "Who exactly are you humans to set yourselves apart from us on the matter of love?"

He looks at me from under his thick, grey eyelashes. "When you say, 'the same as', you imply to me that you think love can be the same as – as what? Love is different in every form, in every moment."

I say, "I'm sorry, but, please, tell me what your people know about love."

"Let us start from one place. We will speak of spatial concepts. Love is complex. It is far more than emotion. You enter a spherical shaped space, and it is turning, moving in motion. You, so to say, step into a bubble, and you step out of your singular dimension. No longer are you one form, but you are as geometry -- remember we aren't yet in emotions in this description of love-- you as body, form, and mind rotating in another vibrancy within a new form. A form of alchemy takes place, which makes you luminous and transparent. Hence the term: being in love. It is transformative. You enter into this other person's place, where hopefully, they are also, entering yours. You speak of a chemical attraction. It is so. If this potion does not work, if the vibrancy of forms doesn't mix, then you experience the falling out, the disappointment, the loss of form awareness.

He continues, "This is geometrical perception, where vast lines stretch into infinity and make up these dynamics of space. Your lines meet, stirring up intensity of form. You either go on together or, the energy of the shapes does not create a new form together."

I keep my eyes focused on a distant point. I do not want him to disappear. This is interesting stuff to me. Love is emotion in my life, not form.

"You can make geometric drawings, and feel what it is like to intersect lines -- when the lines pass each other. In this abstract way, you, nonetheless, can sense the attracting forces that are as lines, in love. You perceive the complexity of love. Two human beings intersect lines, come together into what the human world calls love. In time, these lines move on."

I eye him cautiously. I see a host of other gnomes crowding around him.

He speaks carefully "When you are able to communicate with us, you have drawn a line through our space and crossed over to our lines. We can be together in a new place. Our minds are almost one. We can think to you. However, it took you some years to have courage to talk to us. You must be patient with people in your human kingdom. It is special when friendships happen. Everything in the universe that has creative capacity works on this principle of form and cooperative production.

"When love is between people, look what can be developed. On one hand, you have the family, which comes about through love. Then, you can have people coming together to make new ideas, creations, inventions, vast discoveries, and create out of this love a great harmonious planet.

"When you learn to love, you can learn how to dissipate terror and darkness. That is not yet what we will speak to you about. First is love. If you do not have it, you must seek it. Your life will not be complete without it."

I ask, "What are your families like? Do they live traditionally together as parents, children?

"The older gnomes spend less time with their families. They usually go to the mountains to work underground. They must also learn the magic of our race in order to keep the peace of the forests. Do you know that forests where you walk have magic protecting them? Peace reigns because there is intense training of the gnomes once they have grown their beards. Then they must leave home and tend to other duties. We constantly work to protect what you humans call 'nature'"

I shake my head. I didn't know the forests I loved were peaceful on account of the gnomes.

The gnome family structure seems to work and not break up. Or, did it?

Gnome says," Gnome women hold our families together. Women have a supportive community. They have ways of silently speaking to each other via long distance. They can live at distances from one another, but still be in constant communication. Our women are strong, but they rarely show themselves to humans. Their way of distant speaking is that they think of the person's face and then talk to them quietly."

Gnome continues, "You see, the men leave, as I said, and return at different times of the year. They have strong connections to their families and spouses because they love from their heart. However, the older Gnomes have almost separate societies as they age into very ancient beings. Men and women have quite separate lives."

Laughing loudly, Gnome holds his belly. His eyes sparkle.

"It is good to see you confused. Forget everything I told you, if you want to -- except for one thing. Don't forget that love is action, around you, how you speak, how you sweep a room, how you love an animal. Love is creation."

He says, "Place your hand on your heart and picture it red and feel it beating. Breathe into this beating a rose red fullness, and then picture the world around you as this heart beat. Every step you take, every person you meet, each room of your house, fill with this pulsing living heart. Find a red rose and put one in your own home."

Gnome retreats to where the crickets are calling in the woods. I follow him, talking as I walk.

"At the artist's lecture. new perceptions came to me. You showed me different concepts."

I cannot see him any longer. Then, suddenly, Gnome steps to my side. "I wanted you to sense me, even if you couldn't see me. You see, sometimes I am in constant movement around you, and, other times, I stay behind you."

Birds dart above the water. Insects fly close to the water surface. Children fish at the far end of the pond. There are two bridges over the water at either end. Their grandfather sits on a bench and throws cat food to the fish. I used to talk to him sometimes when I took a walk without the gnomes. Today, I stand apart from the people.

Gnome says, "Today is a fine day. Look at the reed grasses, and flowers. Rest in this. See only what we wish you to see."

I see incredible beauty. I see Little Gnome peek around Gnome.

Gnome tilts his head, "Perhaps, you understand something else?"

Light vibrates off the water, fir tree needles, birch leaves.

"Yes" I say, "I see how the birds dash about. The pond fish can't be seen, but they have produced more fish, or the children wouldn't be fishing. The frogs have multiplied this summer. The flowers are pollinated by insects."

As he searches for a place to sit, he says, "How is it different with people and their activities? We sometimes see unhappy people walking woods. Have they done something wrong, are they moral, or right – they wander in our magic place which is sacred. So often, then, we watch their faces and they are sad, each to themselves, as if their energies had come together for a moment, then dissipated."

I say, "People would be fearful to think you are watching them and there is no true privacy in our world in the forest, or meadows."

Gnome says, "It isn't your world. It is our world. We roam it to protect it. You say, 'our' world. What possessive words are in your world, but of course, we understand. Your world is at a stage of infants, where rules and punishment are needed. I can't expect you to understand a different stage of growth that sometime will happen to the world. Our world, which borders on yours, is simple, as going out into the forest, walking at night through a meadow, lying down in the sweet grasses, breathing in the essence of all things. This is our world. Therefore, of course, we are in it. We watch this world intently, putting in it our love and care. Humans are trespassing in our world." His eyes flash, but the corners of his mouth quiver and he laughs. He lets serious things go by laughing. "Oh, I like that word, 'our'."

Not willing to stop this conversation, I ask him if a couple walks in his woods – what would he say, if they were sad. Would he judge that?

He says, "People are so often not in love, but escaping from the depths of life. That sphere of love, which I described to you, is not with them yet. Their souls are not in alignment. That means their vibrations are very jarred."

"Yeah," I say and watch a butterfly hover on a wild flower.

"Love takes time. Situations stimulate dimensions. Yet, you can meet someone and know instantly you have found lines of energy together. Other people will come to you; you may spend your life with someone, who is not geometrically formed with your soul. You may not experience great love. Some people spend a lifetime searching for love, not realizing they had it and ignored it. They dreamed of a fabulous person to accompany them in life, not seeing that the partner was there as their lesson to learn humbleness, gentle love. Some people find love in old age. It doesn't matter when we find it. It is being aware of knowing we have it."

"If someone hasn't found love and is unhappy, does it mean seeking a new spouse, leaving their family?"

"It isn't always in people that there is great love. Some people find it in passion for their work. Love creates intersecting of infinite lines. Just one of these intersections is one lifetime. You must be content with finding one thing in life you love to do. It will lead you on. However, the focus is in one thing at one time for most people. You would find it hard to have many lovers at a time and to think of that as being fulfillment. However, some people do seek an affair as fresh air, but they don't see its destruction. Those lines of love intersecting get very dim with someone who diverts from a path.

He continues, "With what humans call romantic love -- it is most concentrated and complex when it is in one person. If you leave a love after creating a place together for each other, intricate lines are broken in dimensions. To repair this, you will need to find a new reason for life -- a hobby, a relationship to your own self again."

Gnome sits on a clump of moss. The woods smell damp from a stream.

He speaks, "A painter enters into her painting and she is within a new dimension. She creates because she has let go, explored another imaginative space. It is like a person who is studying. His ideas expand, he thinks hard. He can spend hours exploring ideas and thoughts. He, too, is in another spatial place. A dancer reaches out -- expands into space about her. She works with choreographic form. Watch how her soul leaves her body, enters air, movement. She has to forget herself in her passion of creating to find expression that communicates her feelings."

He is watching ants in the moss. I think about what he had just said.

"Please tell me about the soul of another person."

He never lifts his head, but continues to watch the ants.

"What happens in love completes life. I told you that love is a new dimension. You either fear it, or love it. A mathematical equation is a dimension of form. You can fear the process of solving it, or you can love working it out. It has to be this way. Form without love, is dead. It doesn't create new life. It stays on one dimension. Nothing will work out, without love.

The weather is hot, and I am glad we are sitting under the trees in the shade. After what seems minutes, I wasn't sure I was going to continue this conversation. I wait awhile to listen to a bird calling, and a squirrel scolding.

I decide to ask, "If we aren't operating out of love -- if our life isn't working out -- how can we find this principle of love?"

He spends a few minutes in contemplation. He almost disappears. Little gnome isn't around anywhere that I can see.

Gnome answers, "Life comes in gentle ways. For instance, when you sat by the pond you didn't intend to see the pond in a new way. It became deep, dark -- a sacred place, which you will never forget. In this sacred place is the kernel of creativity. You will return here often to think on this conversation. I won't be with you. You will remember that concepts have no end and thought is an experience. Creating a painting is an experience and that love is the seed you plant when you step back and desire to understand."

I ask, "Is sex apart from the love you speak about?"

"No, but it is separating. It causes pain because it doesn't often accompany a change in consciousness. If there is love -- it has opened you to a further dimension. If a person has sex with someone without this spatial dimension having opened, then it is hard for the relationship to develop. Instead, it is harmful."

I look up into the trees -- it seems our western cultures worship the sexual allurements of women and men. How confusing is this -- to grow up in a world like ours and not learn what is real, enduring about love.

Gnome says, "Love is complex. It contains darkness, but also transcendence. You must ask, what it is to love, and then be able to forgive yourself if love fails.

I ask, "Do these questions exist in your world?"

"Yes, in many forms. I talk to you in your language, what you can understand. I won't be able to find the words in your language to describe my world and its relationships to you."

To my readers – greetings. A whole year passed since writing in this. You can take a break from this, too! But please return! You see, I put my journal and pen on a shelf on the third floor and forgot about them. I was on the phones at work from morning to night, and taking pills for depression. I had no imagination when I took these pills. Then, summer came and finally, I got off them!

August 2001

Days are hot as blackberries ripen. Wind barely rustles the pole beans which stand seven feet high in the garden. Tree leaves crackle. I was troubled, not knowing why. Nature seemed to pick up this dry, rasping sound, as if it would erupt on fire. My thoughts were distracted. I could not keep the gnomes with me, but wandered in my worries elsewhere than where I was -- out in the garden.

Weeds grew among the berry bushes, and I had to pull them off my shirtsleeves. Bugs swarmed around me, but I had a scarf over my head. The berries looked very sweet and I picked just one to eat. Woodland berries taste like the forest, the moss, the meadow and honey all combined.

The Gnomes watch me put them in a bowl. The berry bushes are also seven feet high. They bend away from the sun.

Gnome says, "Slow down as you pick the berries. Observe their colors, the form of each seed. When you have things on your mind, observe each berry so carefully that you feel inside it. You are here, and they are there. You are together. Feel this -- don't think it. Face into the experience. If you stayed all day in the garden, beside this bush, you would be very wise."

I remember shutting my eyes and letting the sun beat on my face.

Gnome said, "These bushes have much to tell you. Ask your questions to them, and they will answer you."

I hold my arms close to me, trying to focus better. I tell the bushes my thoughts, listening for a long time until I answer myself. "Seek solitude," was the answer I tell myself, as if everything for a moment has slipped into place, and I experience quietness. Sitting under a tree, shaded from the heat, we watch the garden and this piece of ground, barely over an acre.

Swimming in a remote Maine lake near us-- I swim at night because the evening is muggy. This is a particular heat that in the north we rarely get. It is the heat coming out of the South. That kind of heat puts people in restless moods. No one had air conditioners in my town. However, this summer a truck rolled in to the Main Street, opened up its back, and sold air conditioners. People shake their heads, saying, "Yep, it's global warming alright."

The sky is full of shooting stars. Let us count all the stars, my father said to me when I was little. He held me high up into the night, as he stood watching the sky, counting as far as we could. Stars had a place in my life, if I counted them. A glittering, silent Universe. How can I forget his face, the smile and belief that sure, we can start counting them.

I swim on my back in the lake, observing the sparkling heaven. The water seems part of the sky. I float among the stars. Mountains, which surround the lake, seem upside down shores. The fishing boats are at a distance. I hear people's voices and sounds of boat motors.

There's a part of the lake to which I swim, and draw a circumference around me of shore and feel myself in the center. To swim in a lake whose water is clear by day so each stone below is seen and by night sparkles with moonlight is an experience to never forget. I am within the earth's womb, her uterus, nurtured and whole. The earth holds me, but I breathe out to the stars. The earth, my mother, keeps my body while my spirit lets go.

I fly out to a part of the sky, a star I call my grandfather. We behold each other. In another group of star clusters are more members of my family. Nothing separates us, for we are now together. I long for them so much in my life, for they were so much a part of my childhood, and now I am, imagining them once more and for a moment, we dwell in each other. This is an incredible feeling to be with my family again.

The hour I float on my back, passes. The moon rises over the fir trees with a shadow of darkness veiling its fullness. The future is in this shadow, I am thinking. It is what we do not know yet. What I would not know then, was that there would be many people departing out of the world and going within these stars, with broken ties to those below. There would be weeping and desperate longing to be with them. Loved ones, we would stretch out to touch just one more time.

My grandmother, Nellie, looks out of the stars as I float on my back. I hear her faint jigging mouth music, and her laughter. I watch her and listen to the motorboats. I had become cold; it was time to return to shore.

I swim towards the dock. The breakwater of rocks juts out, designating the entrance to the village wharf. I pass the rocks.

Waters lap against anchored boats, fir trees let out pollen. Wind blows up to the mountain. A loon calls from a cove. The call sounds like laughter.

"Are you there, Gnome? I ask, for the laughter is his.

"Out here!" comes the call.

"How can I find you out there?"

There is silence. A few minutes pass. Then comes a whisper from somewhere beside me.

"I am here."

Then I laugh to see a small boat made of birch bark drift alongside of me. Inside it sit Gnome and little Gnome. They use sticks as paddles. Moss hangs off the sticks.

"There is one thing you must do. Turn over on your back and look at the sky again."

Doing so, I see how the sky sparkles with flashes through it, as if the stars are shooting out at once. I imagine the sky is a crystal with light shining on it, making it light up. Light is everywhere. The sky looks as a meadow full of white flowers.

The gnome paddles the canoe to the shore and I follow. Getting back energy at the end of each day, is like swimming in a lake, and in the middle you swim slowly because you know you have only so much energy to reach the further shore. It is a sheer effort to make it. I think for some people the end of one's life must feel like this --where it is only the effort to keep living to the last breath and then, the energy wanes, and you lift out of your body, crossing the other shore.

I know I will get through this month of August. It is dry and there is no rain.

Leaves provide shade. Leaning against the tree, I think of my children – I hold them as babies one more time and picture each one. Eleesa in the woven jacket I made her and the plant -dyed woven dress. I spun wool, and dyed it from flowers, apple bark, golden rod, onions, and many other plants. My children and I collected the plants from the meadows, along stream banks. We soaked the wool in the various dyes we made.

Claire, in the handmade dress she loved, with the yellow flowers. Dave in his woolen vest I spun from our sheep, and Polly- who was the one child who wouldn't wear my homemade creations. She wore bathing suits, shorts, one favorite velvet shirt and on her feet, always -- her roller-skates. She skated inside the house, and outside of it. My children come to life in my mind. They play again, and as the wind passing through the forest, their voices rise.

Willing Gnome to come to me, I am aware he stands in the shade.

"You long for the past, but you must live in what surrounds you now."

Nature around me is full of life and movement. Wind lashes through the trees.

Gnome asks, "What do you want?"

"Some sort of adventure."

"I understand. Treasure, however, the moment you are in with your family, friends, nature, and home. Things will change when they are ready. These conversations will pass. If you have lived into each day, worked well even in the job you dislike, you'll find your being positive working with the negative is an energy you create, a protection. You call it hate which you feel, but you merely have to learn to protect yourself – your work is helping you learn this."

I feel guilty for feeling this way.

"Never doubt the moment's relevance. You can experience anger, frustration and set up a positive force rather than connect just to the intellect, which tries to solve problems. Tries," he emphasizes, then chuckles.

"I have been away from you," I say to Gnome. Not only had I been very down but also my body was going through menopause. Tests show my iron count low. I would need another DNC. Unable to contact the gnomes, because of this exhaustion, I put my efforts into getting well. I could barely feed the cats or pat them, make them purr.

Gnome speaks, but I can't see his figure anywhere.

"You are outside yourself, not in tune with what you experience. Hating a job makes you disharmonious. If you like yourself, in every detail, your job wouldn't be so difficult. Your illness makes you irritable and frustrated even more at your job than with your managers and co-workers. You aren't able to be present in your workplace."

"It is so. I snapped out at a manager."

Gnome says. "This might be positive if you live with the emotion and experience its power to change a situation."

I say, "People at work say they're tired. Everyone gets upset at each other, and with their spouses, children at home. I'm not alone."

"Maybe, it is the weather, who knows?" I add.

Gnome holds his knees as he squats on the grass.

"The earth will dissolve -- it has to because it is very old. It is getting tired. It cannot reach its next stage of existence -- everything changes and grows into new forms-- if there is constant war and battles in the world, or even if conflicts exist in a single person. The earth longs for peace in order to transform its energies. It will vanish and we may not realize it has gone, unless we see into it, and observe that life is resting, continuing elsewhere. We call this an interval of time. Chaos is a disharmonious interval of time, but we are moving into this."

I feel intense electricity in the air. My scalp tingles, my hands prickle, as if a thunderstorm is near.

I ask, "So we are responsible for our peace and the earth's harmony together- they both go together?"

"Yes. You can be active in different ways. Meditation is the deep state of concentration on peace. Prayer connects you to Spirits that need you."

I look at the garden close beside me. Squash leaves and flowers sprawl from their bed on to the lawn.

I say, "There are some plants that make me feel sad. They symbolize the end of summer and I can't bear that this season is over soon."

Gnome, looking out to the woods, says, "These are the plants which you need. In this end of summer, the turmoil you experience will be with these plants. It makes you reflective, and gives you strength."

Night comes with a chilly wind, despite the day's heat. I think about August nights when I camped in the woods with my cousins, and heard deer snorting in the forest. We shivered in our sleeping bags and watched the stars. In the morning, we'd run into the warm kitchen and crowd around the cooking wood stove. Days and nights in the mountain woods as summer changed to autumn, contained acute sense awareness. The smells of the pine trees as dusk came, the cough of a deer -- such memories come to me tonight.

Gnome is quiet beside me. I am listening to how day shifts into evening. The crickets start up almost as the birds sleep. He seems to reflect on night.

"Listen to the crickets. Some are very fast in their sounds, others slow. What else do you feel about the night-- you can live in the darkness; watch the shooting stars fly across the sky... Does this quiet you, the night sky turning colors above you?"

I close my eyes, hearing the crickets, smelling the moss, and fir trees. Dampness rises from the forest and pond. I draw in deep breaths. Yes, I calm down. I realize how long it has been since I have slept outside with only a sleeping bag under the stars.

A bird calls one last song. Night arrives.

"Remember yourself as a child, how happy and carefree you were. Don't forget this. What do you picture when you listen into night?" Gnome asks.

I was a child, running in the meadows chasing fireflies with my siblings. My parents gave us glass jars to keep them in, like lanterns. Then, happy and tired, we'd sit down to a bowl of cereal, then go to bed., our fireflies sparkling in the canning jars beside us. When we slept, my father would take them out, and release them to the dark sky. He was careful to tend to life. If we were still awake, then my mother and father sang us songs to get us to sleep.

"What songs?" he asks.

"The world's songs -- comforting songs, melancholic ones; they were songs my parents loved. Their love for them mattered most."

Gnome looks into the distance. Maybe he is remembering his childhood.

"What do you see?"

I tell him, "I picture a bird flying west, into the sunset."

"Think on that bird. The bird will take you out of exhaustion," says Gnome.

Gnome is outside wandering somewhere else than near me, in the transition of August to September. His silence disturbs me. It mirrors summer changing into autumn. I long for summer to remain, but nights advancing onwards, will be getting cold. Then, this year, the woods going into autumn are too dry. The drought makes mellow color tones: trees have muted yellows, reds, and orange leaves. Rain is needed.

I asked the gnomes why they were distant. They showed me an electrical field all around and they could not step into our world. On the edge of the fields were jagged forms as if they were daggers and I withdrew in alarm, thanking them for being able to show me this, for it seemed painful to them. They could not speak to me.

After work, I went out in the woods and listened to the trees and what they said was this--that they come to people who work with their challenges, and don't give up. Each tree has different beings, sometimes multitudes of beings within one tree, as a totem pole has many faces. Each time

I want to leave my work, the tree beings appeared to me, beseeching me to remain and work things out.

Gnome and Little Gnome sit on my desk. They were intensely fascinated with machines and the people staring at them. If I looked up, saw them there, and asked them for help, they only sent me thoughts -- to dig in. To be in everything I do. Be in the computer's workings. Gnomes were positive about most everything. Even with corporations such as the one I worked in, they were curious about technology.

Although after work, when I was very tired, they were distant from me in conversation, they were somewhere not too far from me, because I felt them as circles of warmth.

September 2001

Mabel said she was off- going up to Cape Breton for several weeks. She walked into my kitchen, saying "hi," and then had gone over to the refrigerator door to look at what was hanging on it. She liked to stand in front of my refrigerator and stare at what was beneath the magnets.

The door has news articles – some of them are mine I occasionally write for a local paper - and photos of children over it. That morning, the last I ever saw her, she turned away from the refrigerator and asked me to go with her. I wish, I had said yes to her, but I shook my head. That would be impossible, to get excused from work so suddenly. Now I have to regret for my whole life not going.

"That awful job: you must find a better one," she had said. She sighed and gave me a very huge hug; I was startled because Mabel rarely hugged people. She said thank you so much for helping me with music. I shook my head, saying, but we have lots more work ahead of us. Then, she smiled and got into her car.

Things started happening. I got a phone call at the end of the first week of September, saying Mabel fell off a cliff in Cape Breton, and died. I journal this in a different notebook. I was deep in grief.

Then, six days later, planes hit the World Trade Center. I journal this, too, along with writing about Mabel. I let out my emotions on sheets of paper I never looked at again. I had to do it this way, not here, in this journal. There was close grief for Mabel, and abstract grief, a communal grief of the nation.

When they found Mabel, crabs had eaten her. Drifting in the sea, lost for many days a fisher- man spotted her. Before they knew she had fallen, she was simply missing. Her children had looked for her, given up, and then finally when they got home, back here, heard the news of her body found. I received a postcard from her after her death, written before her cliff hike. She wrote that she had been singing. I feared she'd been singing on cliff edges. Before she left for Cape Breton, after our last music lesson, I'd told her how I loved to sing beside the sea. So was I to blame for her accident? I feared so, yet- who knows. I heard later that others also blamed themselves for aspects of Mabel's death.

In going through a box Mabel had in her car, I learned she had studied Gaelic as a student at Radcliffe College years ago. She still remembered how to pronounce the language, and certain words in our songs. We had songs planned for autumn to learn. She had intense joy in these. Along with discovering her ability to sing, she was strengthening her ankles so she could hike again. I regret that I hadn't had the courage to say to my managers I had to take personal leave to go with her to Cape Breton. I believe she lost her balance and fell. Others think she committed suicide.

After the events of Mabel passing and 9/11, I continued to watch for the Gnomes to come back. The world seemed blazing up around me. Mabel's son- in- law, who has a branch of the Bread and Puppet Theater, near here, produced a play called, "When the World was on Fire." We acted in it. The audience was packed. We were thinking of Mabel watching, removed from pain, and the destruction in New York City.

End of September 2001

Gnome sits on the porch or is off in the forest. I hope he is waiting for me to feel better. I only see what needs doing in front of me and conversations tire me. The world of work, and my home are vastly different from each other and my small world is barely surviving.

I sit in the garden to find peace. I feel rewarded if the gnomes come to watch this garden. Sometimes they get up in a fruit tree. I think, oh, Gnome and Little Gnome have been around me and I am blind to them. Little Gnome stays very much in the background, and I don't mention him very often. He is listening to everything.

The garden has many tomatoes and pumpkins. We have not picked them. Eggplants, shining in purple, ripen. Squash leaves -- large, spreading over the garden bounds. Standing to look at this, I imagine plants are able to communicate together. What would they talk about? Cucumbers, zucchini, beans, peas tumble over, excited to be alive.

When I go to Mabel's, walking around her garden, I miss her presence in her home, and don't feel anymore that I could just walk in and say hi -- to the rest of her family who live there. Her daughter keeps up her garden.

Sitting by the herbs, I look out on the mountains. The vision of the man telling me everything would change has come true. Yet as much as change has altered my relationship to Mabel's home, I look out now to the mountains surrounding it. New York was far from here. I could hear Mabel saying, you are safe in these mountains.

I tell each plant in her garden that she had gone; she was with the others who have passed onwards. I go by her tomatoes, flowers, then out of the garden into the orchard, looking at each fruit tree. I taste an apple, which has fallen to the ground. Bees swarm over the fruit.

I say, "Bees, Mabel has passed on. I remember reading how rural English people told their bees when someone had passed on. Bees, they said, were close to the Dead.

Her daughter walks around her gardens. Mabel's family has asked me to play music for her funeral. It is hard to sing. Sadness encompasses the entire room.

After the service, a turkey vulture flies overhead, circling for a long time. Someone says the bird is Mabel. No one moves until it flies west.

The sun rises from the forest. Heavy shadows linger in the yard. Slowly, the dawn lightens the garden. Looking out to this delicate light from my bedroom window, I imagine I see an angel. I think on Mabel and long to call her back from another world. Thinking on her sudden, tragic death, I question each moment of her fall from a cliff. I ask myself did death come quickly, or did she suffer? Did she float in the sea for a while, gazing to the sky, or choke on the salt, stinging water? Did her life flashback in her, as they say happens on sudden death, or what – what was her soul experiencing?

Did she scream as she fell? What was it like to trip and slip from a high cliff path into the sea? Would she have known that her precious body was found after five days by the angler who will never forget finding her?

My father had a friend who was making these trails in Cape Breton. He, also, died on the pathways there. They are not easy paths. The hiker trespasses into the world of wildness. Beings who pull him off his path, into a void. You can fall, die of heart attack alone out there. Maybe Mabel fainted, or her heart failed her.

I fall back on my pillow, and sleep again. Then, on waking, it was as if she were close beside me, wishing me to get up. She wants to sing. I lift my head from the pillow, but I am not able to sing. I lie back again. What is this feeling of communication, between sleep and waking, with Mabel? I began to talk with her, silently sending thoughts to her. It seemed the gnome had helped me in a new kind of communication with the Invisible where one can silently speak with others who are at a distance.

She asks me, "Is it everything the same with you? Are you are alright?"

I tell her about 9/11. She had grown up in that city, and her family still kept an apartment there.

"Mabel, it is not the same. Airplanes, piloted by 'terrorists' hit the twin towers in the city, near to your apartment. The towers fell and many people died. Dust covered everything in your apartment. Up in the mountains, in your home, everything is almost the same, but you are gone and we miss you."

"I'm not happy I caused grief," Mabel says.

"I know -- I'm sorry too."

She seems to reflect.

"It's only that many people love you, Mabel."

She looks up. "They do?"

"They do, Mabel."

"I don't know why..." her voice trails off as if she had vanished.

"You can lie down beside me here, share my pillow, Mabel. My cat is beside me on the other side of the pillow. We're still sleeping. Not time to get up. It's hardly day."

She lies down with the cat and I return to sleep. When I awake she is gone, and I nearly forgot this conversation because I jumped up to let the cat out the door.

Sometimes I think how Mabel didn't realize how people loved her, because she concentrated on how she loved them. Vince, her neighbor, told me she had come to his house in the last months. She'd call out, "Just coming in, Vince is everything okay?" He'd say that yes, everything was fine. Then she would leave, not saying goodbye. You know, he said, spacey like. Before Mabel left for Cape Breton, he asked her again.

"Hey, do you mind me asking why you come into my house like this, not saying what you are doing, taking one look at me and asking, am I okay?

Mabel had said to him, "Oh, I am only checking up on you, Vince, just making sure you're alright." Vince then understood that she'd heard he'd had heart trouble and was concerned about his health.

At another time, she came into his house, and said, "Vince, you wouldn't mind if I sit down and have a good cry?"

"No, Mabel. Sit down. What is the matter?" he asked. She sat at his kitchen table.

She cried, a rare thing to see from Mabel. "My family is angry with me."

"Why, Mabel?"

"About money, Vince." She didn't say more than that. They didn't approve of how much she helped low income families by giving them things they needed. Mabel was a legend in the back woods.

"They're not going to keep that up, with her gone – nope. That is at an end," he had said, referring to the rest of her family. Mabel gave, with no wish to have the money returned.

In the Other World, the Television World, the incidents of 9/11 are taking their toll. People watch TV non-stop. They are stressed, my work place is on fire, strained. In the non TV World, mine – because I'm too busy to watch it, there is a lot of gossip.

For instance, someone I work with said two of the terrorists passed right by our workplace on the way south from Canada. They stopped at a store near us and no one realized this until they were dead and recognized in photos. Still, the world outside my town did not enter my life too much.

My thoughts are often not on the nation's sorrow. I hide this as guilt assails me of not maybe caring enough because no one I know, or so I thought, met their death.

I miss playing music with Mabel, and her loving spirit on earth. It is hard to reconcile her tragic death with goodness -- the great love she felt for people.

Even though there is talk she had committed suicide, I was not sure she had. I keep going over the last moments with her, and what she spoke about, just before leaving for Cape Breton. I repeat it to myself. She had made plans for the autumn. She had to be at a county fair because of being in charge of a booth on supporting local gardeners, crafters, in short, handmade local economy.

I go over the songs we had planned to learn. She wanted her daughter to come to the singing. She had even asked me to go to Cape Breton with her. Did this point to suicide?

When I turn news on to the events of 9/11, I am swept into a national sorrow, but nothing that is exactly personal. I read the daily NY Times – none of us can afford that paper so we go to the local library each day to read it- and the articles on the lives of each missing person. I scour the names for people I might know. No one yet. I look hard at newspaper photos. I want to immerse myself in this grieving process of the country, too, as well as my personal grieving for Mabel.

My daughter phoned to say a person she worked with had a husband on the airplane that went down in Pennsylvania. Before the plane went down, her husband phoned to say goodbye. He said they were trying to gain control of the airplane from the hijackers. Then, while on the phone, his wife heard a huge explosion and communication was cut off. She was called by the military and told the plane was shot down because they knew it was on route to the White House.

Gnome sits in the garden. Been awhile since a conversation. He says, "Relate to your life: taking care of the garden and making bread."

My mind is still almost totally occupied with Mabel. I'd like to ask Mabel, as if she were standing at my refrigerator door, "Where are you now? There is such a mess that happened after you died." Someone said she'd be down in New York City, digging in the rubble, trying to find survivors. She loved this city, as she did the mountains. She'd awake one morning to the idea of it, and would have gotten into her Subaru and driven down.

At her grave the minister read, "Think not of tomorrow ... for the morrow will take thought of the things of itself." That was my experience of her. For her, each day gave her new ideas, things to do, people to drop in on, like Vince, and a song to work on with me.

She'd had an idea to learn to sing. She knocked on my door, and asked me if she could do so. I said, or course. We went to a local bakery and talked over hot soup. After that, she came to my house once a week. We went through many songs. She didn't think she could sing at age 69. I told her she could. I played the music on my recorder, before singing it. She told me she'd like to sing in Gaelic.

After the funeral, and an informal gathering at her home, I went over to her grave and watered the plants. I sang what we had worked on in Gaelic. I tried to remember the right accents and dynamics of the words. I released my grief into the singing. She was pleased to have mastered this song. I sang some more – especially Gaelic lullabies and work songs.

Where she rests, the grave looks out to the mountains, the same ones she looked on from her home. I planted more flowers for her. Her children seemed to forsake her grave, so I didn't burden them with my grief, or how I sit by her to sing and water the plants. I began to read about grief, and how I can't fight it, but allow it to be with me, and it can take years to dissolve.

I didn't know then, that my mother and father's passing in the near future, would be the hardest for me to bear, and when they died, I would be able to let Mabel go, except that I always returned to Mabel's grave because it was so near in proximity to me, in order to plant the flowers each spring and sing the Gaelic for her. With my mother, I grieved for a relationship I had longed to make closer. To mend the outer and to reassure myself the inner, the love between us was what mattered no matter how much we quarreled; there was love. With my father, a love so deep, that he was my teacher of nature, of life, of friendships. He was not perfect, but he never swore, and he was only angry with me two times in my life – when I backed his little VW bug into a fence post of our pony field. When I nearly stripped the gears as I drove down a mountain in Vermont.

Often now, in the lovely meadow graveside beside the mountain near Mabel's, I think on her special qualities. I wonder if Gnome misses her and visiting her home. He respected how she listened to people and murmured her encouragement to them, but rarely spoke of herself. She'd say to them, "That sounds great. Can you, somehow, do it?" You found yourself saying, "Sure, I can do it." After she left, you'd start figuring out how to do it, like you'd made her a promise.

Red maples contrast dark green fir trees. Autumn is here. Despite the lingering warmth of each day, we burn the stove. At night, crickets call. Their song is a steadfast beat, keeping summer alive. The moon is half-full. Rain and mists come move like a blanket over trees, blocking stars.

Cats sleep on the sofa by the stove. I go out to walk barefoot in the damp grass. In the season moving in, wishes overwhelm me: summer to last, autumn to linger because of its beauty.

My work place is in shock of 9/11, but I am weeping over Mabel. Her death and the suffering seems only a breath away. A sigh, or line of music, bring thoughts of Mabel and more tears.

Since Mabel's death, I stopped singing. Did I need a reason to stop? Did Mabel's passing fill my need? I don't think so. I felt finished with performing, at least until grief left me. In stopping performing, I could look on nervous energy as a stranger now. Before a performance, I had large tensions, and I let them create my energy on stage, and I enjoyed being with an audience, creating a mood with song.

How will I ever sing again with this pain? I speak to Mabel, as if she is sitting in my home and that she, being in the wide universe, can look out and answer me from the stars.

Gnome sits on the sofa and I stand in the doorway talking to him. It is fresh air to have him with me, like old times. "I am blaming myself that I didn't go to Cape Breton with Mabel. She might not have fallen off the cliff had I been with her. She had weak ankles, Gnome."

He says, "In time she will be free. She ties to earth because we are sad about her. She misses her family. Think on her. Think of how she feels. It is sad to be lost from the earth not understanding what happened. She did not expect to fall."

As I mentioned before, a number of her friends think she took her life. I don't believe she did, because of how happy and excited she was becoming about life, her body, singing and community, and the future songs we had planned for autumn.

Gnome says, "Sing to Mabel, even if she is gone. Keep her in memory."

I imagine her with me, sitting down for a music lesson. Her expression is worried. I ask her, "What is the matter, Mabel?" She answers, "I am tired. Her voice fades.

"Where are you?" I ask. "There are forms which shift about and melt away, reappear again."

She says that it's a fresh feeling, being out of her body, like watching the sunrise -- where winds blow and she is in them. She is learning to accept this, but it is different.

I try to sing what she learned before going to Cape Breton. I stop in the middle of it.

"I miss you, Mabel, as my student. A teacher needs a student, as much as the student needs the teacher." She looks for a long moment at me.

As I talk with her, (this silent talking which relieves my sorrow), the Gnome is listening.

I say to Mabel, "If you see me, the way I see you,(as in memory), then you must want me to keep talking or singing, but I have to stop. I am tired. I have talked to 1000 people this week at my job."

She sits at a different angle from Gnome. She and he blend in silent communication. Together they vanish. The room has only dark brown furniture in it, so old that my great grandfather once sat on the chair here.

Winter coming 2001

On another day, Gnome returns. He is with me as I stoke the stove. The wood, some of it cut from our trees, is stacked in cord lengths in the barn. In New England, old houses have a door from the home into the barn. You bring wood in without getting on your boots.

This house is large. When we thought of selling it and moving away, Mabel had always talked me into staying. She believed in possibilities. Think up something new. If you aren't making headway, change course. Live in cold rooms, she said. Bundle up.

Mabel liked winter, although she never told me she did. She wore old boots, with laces often undone. She took her time going over snow, careful not to fall on ice. She waddled from side to side as she went on a pathway. Looking up, she'd smile when someone inched by.

She loved the holiday season. The Christmas tree stood in the large room in her house. The fireplace glowed with a huge log. Friends gathered and sat by the fire, holding potlucks for any reason they could find. In the holiday season, music filled her house, but she didn't sing. She was shy about this.

She was beginning to get bolder about the thought of singing. In each song session, I told Mabel that her voice was getting stronger. She said the problem was, she couldn't hear her own tones with many people singing around her. She thought she wasn't singing the right notes. We worked together to make sure she heard the right tones, and then sang them in the key as she heard them. When she sang alone, she gained confidence.

Gnome sits in my room. Here, where in reality, Mabel is memory, and imagination draws her back to me, I feel her beside us. I ask gnome if he feels it.

Rising from the rug, he moves to a chair, where Mabel used to sit.

This remembrance of Mabel, which seems such a real presence, comes in. I silently think to her, "Listen to the silence and sing out of it. What do you hear tonight, Mabel?

She says to my thoughts, "I hear a cricket."

Deep in Winter 2001

When I feel the presence of another realm, where quietness permeates a space, the beloved departed are close. It is as if they lean to touch my shoulder. This presence of peace, I think is what the Dalai Lama asks us to be present within. He urges us to find the wish to have peace and happiness to our home. It is a great gift if we are able to do this. We can be downcast, argumentative, or we can flip the coin and live for peace.

Gnome is at peace. His presence is so firm, strong and he is sure of himself. The gnome listens to the conversations of my family at home, and watches the cats. His being in the home make me feel the essence of why we live together as a family, and to be thankful we are together.

If you can see him, he says, he likes to look through your heart. The heart reaches out. It is the same with other creatures. A smile warms them.

Mabel drifts in as a ghost feather blowing, landing on the ground. The curtain slightly moves as if a wind stirs. Gnome sits and listens to Mabel saying she is back for a music lesson. She collapses in the chair.

"Are you really here?" I say to her. "Can I believe it is true?"

Despite my disbelief, I start to sing. She sings back the Gaelic words to the tune. She sings with light shining on her face. When I think on how she loves music, I feel badly that I want to stop playing, give it a break for a while -- which I will do, for some years.

Still, I promise her that each day for a while, just in this room alone together, we will sing. Our music will be only for us. There won't be an audience or friends listening.

Gnome frowns, because he likes people to be merry, and get over things. His frown makes me laugh. He wears green pants, brown jacket, and a floppy velvet green hat, which hangs over his bushy eyebrows. His outfit makes me smile.

Mabel wears a blue skirt, long shirt and old sneakers. Her white hair is back casually as ever... She is beautiful, only more radiant, rested, than on earth. She tells me how her fall off the cliff was terrible. She felt that all the bones in her body were crushed. It was as if she were all broken.

She drifts off out the window. Gnome and I wait, thinking she hasn't finished her visit yet. After some time, she comes back.

She shakes her head, as if to dry off her hair. "It is all over."

"You mean death, Mabel?" I ask.

She nods. For a while she is silent. "Death...it was nothing at all. Nothingness."

I ask, "Do you feel better now? Do you have the sense of the World where you are?"

"Yes. There is light. It is very special... it is fine, really... but I miss my family so much...I wish they knew I am often with them. My spirit floats beside them on the earth. In this sense I am back with them. I had to be absent for awhile to get another orientation in my new world."

"Do you know you were an angel to me, on earth, Mabel? You brought me so much by your presence in my home. It was beautiful how much you loved to sing."

"Me - an angel?" She seemed aghast at this thought.

December 2001

Winter blows hard winds and ice covers the trees, and the woods tighten with cold. Darkness is heavy. Night comes about 4:30 pm. Year in and out, I leave work when it is dark; go to work just as daylight breaks. This year snow has been scarce and Gnome is away more often.

My job got extra hard after the events of September. The stress levels of people, especially management, are high. Now, even more, no one likes going to work. When we call people, they are rude, and not happy. No one wants to talk about money; sales are down. We talk about 9/11 with our customers, not about the products we sell. Management says it is okay to discuss life, not money – anything to keep customers on the phones with us. And every topic comes back to September 11.

At work, I called a customer who had lost her daughter in the World Trade Center. I talked to another man, a firefighter from the city, who had stayed home from work that day, and now feels terrible that so many of his friends died. He felt lost, he said. He could see the towers falling from his apartment window.

I come home worn out. I don't cry for anyone but myself, needing change. I realize harmony is far from me. I look for the gnomes, but can't find them.

Mabel's daughter is shopping in town, and I ask her if it is going to be hard this Christmas. I felt, now, we are moving on, and talking at least, about her family.

She replies that there is much to do. They had gone to New York City, where Mabel grew up, and stayed a month, and yes, they had been to ground zero. The apartment of Mabel, near to it, was thick with dirt and dust. She didn't say anything more. She was looking for stocking gifts. I ask one more thing: did she get to dance in the city -- Mabel's daughter is a dancer -- Yes, she told me she had attended a workshop in the Village. That is good. She is doing something for herself.

Her husband tries on boots. We don't talk about Mabel. They say I should come over and play music. I say, thanks – maybe soon, being polite, knowing I won't. Whenever I had gone over to Mabel's it was to play music for her. Her children, grandchildren were in and out of the house, but never listening for long. I have no reason to go any longer.

I finger the woolen socks. Socks mean warmth. I look across the aisle at the boot rack. Boots mean comfort -- dry feet. Perhaps, Christmas is about symbols of what we ordinarily use. It is not about the buying -- although everyone is saying to spend to keep the local economy going.

Gnome returns. Cold comes with snow and winds. Last winter had large drifts banked against the first floor windows. Gnome slowly walks into the room.

I do not want Gnome to settle back into a chair and be comfortable here. I want to go with this energy of change. I feel like moving onward, quitting my job, skiing into the backcountry.

When you are on medicine for depression and you want to not ever take it again, because your hair falls out, and your eyes cannot stand the sun – and because visions get blocked by such medicine – then, you got to take what the Universe gives you. Gnome is a friend. I want him to ski into the forest.

Gnome knows I would call my manager and leave a message saying I am done – finished with my job. I might change my mind, put on my skis, and head out into the night. He watches me as the woodstove burns and the cats sleep.

"Make some tea. Bring me a cup. We'll watch the fire and stoke it all night."

Night takes long to leave. The cat raced around as if chased by the elves. I did not quit the job, and in the early morning, took my skis on a back trail and did not get lost.

Elves are creatures that observe Gnome and me from the corners of the room, from under chairs, sofas, behind curtains, in closets. They sit on cellar stairs. I have not spoken much to them, for they rarely carry words inside of them. They are in activities, either helping or being up to pranks. They like to be impish, and if a cup falls on the floor, not to mind. It is their pranks, and if you laugh it off, they will not repeat their mischief.

Snow is a foot deep. The wood's trails are covered. I haven't skied at night in the forests for a long time and I am glad I didn't try it the other night, because we have a mountain lion out there and by day we track its prints and tail marks.

Gnome is on top of my grandmother's treadle sewing machine. He likes old furniture that has been in the family. Each item holds memory. He remembered my Grandmother sewing, bending over the machine, and he wishes me to think of her and maybe even use the machine again.

"What would that create? " I ask.

"Will power in you."

"Sewing?"

"The energy you get from sewing is attention to detail."

I remember when I made my clothes and it made me think of being spontaneous, deciding on something I liked, then making it. I took time to think on this, and the gnome watches me

He says, "So, you are thinking about your old self?"

"Yes, but it is distant from me."

"But you are happy for a moment. Your eyes light up. Remember how you were like this when you were young."

I remember a verse I had written to myself to inspire me when I was young. I recite it to Gnome:

Come back to feeling with me,
I am the spirit of the wind,
I blow and yet you fight my soul;
I am your life, your strength,
to climb the mountain side alone.

He asks where I had written this. I tell him in a car, when I was with friends when I was eighteen. We were heading out west to live on Vancouver Island, B.C.

He says it is a power verse. It is for my life.

I tell him that when I was out west I was terribly homesick for the forests of the northeast and the mountains.

He says, "You are having a hard time with winter right now."

He asks me to think back on two days ago, and what happened for me at work.

"You went to work with me. You sat on my desk and watched me make calls all day. You told me I couldn't talk to you at work. That if I stared into space, silently talking to you, it wouldn't look good for me. Then you told me why I was having a hard time at my job."

"What did I tell you?"

"I was very out of myself. I needed to make a boundary and work within it. I had to define exactly what I had to do, and how to say it. I had to get back my selling technique which I had lost since September 11."

"And when I said this to you, what did you see around you?"

"I saw a battlefield. I saw myself out in a place of havoc, confusion, hurt and pain, and it all entered into me, causing me to lose my style of selling at work. You showed me why I couldn't make my sales anymore."

"And... have you done anything about it?"

"I have tried," I replied.

"Goodnight." He jumps off the sewing machine and points to the light. I turn it off.

In his absence, I reflect on the day backwards, from the end to the beginning, about my day job, how I cannot do it, yet I continue because it is for my family. I remind myself to always keep this in mind; be thankful for what you got, gal. Here in this small town, jobs are scarce.

The cat gets up, opens the china closet door and goes inside it. It is warm in there because the closet sets against the old brick chimney. I wish I could fit in there with the cat and the elves. The radio says the night will go below zero. I stoke up the woodstove, and head to the cold bedroom.

February 2002

Snow keeps falling. A foot turns into feet. People are silent. Then the sky opens. Moonlight shines down on the snow, stars glitter. The air lifts.

Sunrise colors are deep orange. The trees glow in this color. "Red in the morning, shepherds' warning," my mother would say to me. In the Swiss Alps, close to where I once lived, I had looked out the window to see the alps red, on fire, the meadows bursting with this color. Frightened, I closed the curtains. The cattle were out in these high meadows. They were not reacting to this color as I.

Today is such a morning. Is this a warning to one's day? Bad weather is coming. I dig a hole in the snow to sit and read. A friend who is a healer told me three things help depression. Sun, rest and water. I make this hole and feel the sun's warmth. I have a bottle of water. The sun is strong, as on a beach in summer.

After sitting for a couple hours there, I stretch. I call it snow bathing to my friends at work. They say my face looks fresh. My manager says she likes the idea. It is better than a tanning bed.

Gnome is by the stove, when finally I get cold enough and go inside. I am glad. I want to talk to him.

"Last winter you told me to be in things, live into them. What do you think of this winter, is it the same?"

"This winter you must be as air, imagine yourself light, without gravity. You have the weight from last winter's work, the gravity from being within objects. That which surrounds what you were within last winter, feels as air. Be in it."

These are two polarities. Feeling within substance, seems heavy. Putting myself into the air, is lightness. I get warm beside the stove and then return to my snow hole. I watch shadows sliver across the snowfield.

Gnome joins me there. He says, "Imagine yourself going out into the distance, picture yourself doing this."

I expand as if there are wings on me. I enter a dimension of finer ether.

I read at the table, beside the fire. Then, pull out the bills. Paper clutters my dining room table. With doing the bills on this table, Gnome doesn't have a place to sit. I need to clear some space so he can get up and kick his legs.

He stands beside me with his arms crossed. He wears a green velvet jacket with white fur lining, well-worn leather boots, and the hat that resembles a crown.

He says, "You race through your day."

"I have to race home from work, so I can do a few things before it is time to sleep again. My day is very organized!"

He shakes his head, "Quite the opposite. Your day is chaos. You are in it, but you seek to be outside of it. You can't connect to it. You tear around inside your mind, creating another kind of chaos. Slow down."

I put a red velvet cushion on a stool. He sits on it, changing his position to get comfortable, like a cat or a dog will do, and then, he swings his legs. He keeps on the coat with the white fur inside it, but he has switched to another hat. He has found a brown one with a white feather sticking out of it.

"How do you change hats so quickly?" I ask.

"It's imagining what we want to wear. Also, I think you like this hat with the owl's feather, right?"

Aunt Eileen, Nana Nellie's daughter, shook her head over the fickleness of the Little People. They loved many outfits. They wore colors and clothes she liked – artist's berets and smocks, and they walked around with paintbrushes. This way, they knew they'd make her laugh.

Gnome insisted on having a cup of tea. I left some in my cup for him. I remember how Nana used to do this. Leave a little bit in the cup, dearie, for the little folk, I can hear her say. Telling the day from the tea leaves in her cup made her have to drink several cups of tea. After she had prophesized the day – only then, she poured out a second cup for the Little People.

When Gnome showed up, I set out his tea. Holding our hot mugs, we observed each other. I liked him there, a comfortable presence, when the stove burned slowly, and the house was silent and everyone slept.

Tonight I ask him, "Do you remember me making tea for you with sugar?"

The fire flames shine out from the cracks in the old Irish stove. I put more wood on the stove, stoking it up for the night. I look sideways at Gnome.

He says, "You are silly. Of course, I remember. I have the memories of centuries ---of having tea with your ancestors."

I am very silent at that. He seems impatient with me lately.

"Why are you impatient with me?" I can see him look around the cluttered dining room covered with paper work, especially bills, over the table. We shove the bills out of the way to eat.

"Nothing is in its place."

He sounds like my mother. Only she gave up with me. She rarely visited my home, overwhelmed at how messy it was. I could not please her easily. I am sad about it now. I should have done this or done that, I say, but then, I chose not to pick that battle, for I didn't have the time for constant tidying up, and I didn't have the money to hire someone to do it.

Gnome persists. I tell him that the clutter began when I started working full time.

He says, "I don't feel invited, welcomed or comfortable in your home. Today, you took the screwdriver, which has been sitting on the coffee table since Christmas, and put it away. That is a relief!"

I ask, "Does one thing like that matter so much?"

"Of course, it does. Leaving items around is like leaving part of you. Now, by putting the screwdriver away, you will find the next thing to do. Your bills will get paid, too."

He walks into the living room, stares at the books piled on the floor and sheets of music fallen off the piano (knocked over by the cat) and not picked up. These piles of music which I need to put away -- somewhere.

He sits on another disheveled table and says he changed his mind just now. He likes some of the mess, saying he loves it when music mess is what I keep around me. I have been trying to work on playing music again.

"I like this room because you are working at what you love. We can sit here, and have our tea and conversation."

There isn't a space for tea cups. I tell him, that I have to start cleaning up, because I am trying to find my tuning key.

"You could try looking in the barn." He is joking, of course. My tuning key would not be in the barn. The barn is an enormous project to clear up. If I try to find something in our barn, I will need a truck to clear it out and take the mess to the dump.

He may be joking, but he hits a truth. As he sits on the piano stool, he swings his legs very rapidly. The cat on the sofa stretches into a new position on a blanket. She sits up, turns around, yawned, sees nothing, and lies down again.

I tell him, "I am forever wishing, each day, that I could leave my job."

"You are impatient. Your job is a relationship to something, and to people. In your case, it is mostly to people. If you wish to move on, you must figure out why all the people you work with are with you in time, this time in space, and what you need to resolve with each person. Maybe it is a smile at them, instead of a frown. Yes, I know you've been trying to laugh more at work and lighten up, but don't ignore the people. Every single person who is seated next to you by your manager is a relationship you need to meet and fulfill, and sometimes a simple thing as a smile resolves this."

I have never thought the solution to job discontent is that simple -- to work on relationships with people. Never mind the job, computers I do not like, the constant push to please our customers.

I say, "So you are saying, find out who the person is sitting beside me and try not to ignore my managers. Yea, they are people. (Most of the times they are like barking dogs)."

Gnome says, "It's the lesson you have to learn."

He gets up and walks around the room, picking up a book, putting it down. He continues, "You have to overcome obstacles. You are meeting people in a very materialistic computerized environment whose energy fields blocks out clarity of who a person really is. Years ago, think on it, you'd never have these machines and cubicles in between you and others."

I say, "You have to come to work with me again. When you are there, however, I can't find a way to talk with you because I am so busy on the phones. You suddenly arrive. You sit on top my desk and I wonder how you got past security, but then, you can go through anything."

He takes it seriously. "There are two people in there who know me. I have watched them while passing through the front doors. Their eyes widened. They could be too much for you, for even though they can see into another dimension, they don't trust what they see, so they will take extra precaution to make sure they make your life difficult. They won't trust you. I will be careful not to show myself to them again. They are the security guards at the front desk. I have to be careful."

At this I laugh, thinking he pulled my leg. I assure him he is welcome to visit me at work. I did not think he could help me with making sales better. It seems that no one can give me advice, and I was now constantly unable to meet my daily sales quotas. I constantly remembered the days when I did very well and was number two in the company at sales. After 9/11, despite our efforts to get up to get sales back up high, I was not alone in struggling with lower performance records. The managers stressed over this, and they blamed us. It is your tone of voice, or it's how you talk to the customers. Talk to them, ask them about their day, see where you can find a need to a product you are selling, the managers said. It was good advice, in normal situations, but the economy is bad. It is not our approach.

Spring 2002

Gnome meets me in the woods. Snow melts; ground underneath thaws. As I walk, I wonder, will I expand the herb garden, or keep it in its present shape? Instead of making it larger, maybe it only needs a new path. After our walk in the woods, I sit beside the herbs, hoping they will grow well into summer.

We jump over snow to clear patches of ground. We find the stream, which runs from the pond through a dip in the woods, underneath ground and into another field. It had been a rushing stream, but changed its course. It goes eastward, instead of south. There are other feeder streams into the east stream and it will fill with melting snow soon, and course around the stones and make them angry, for they remember the time when the brook went in the southerly direction.

I tell Gnome it's been a tough week.

He says, "You are worried about how the course of things change, and that weeks don't go as planned. With a change of direction, you have to make sense of what you see, even if you can't understand how things changed."

"I am blaming myself for feeling impatience with my life." I don't give him details. He shakes his head.

He says, "You took leaps of faith and trust and this generates something more than the material. You must know this. You must not blame yourself for the courage you took to act, or speak from your heart because your intentions are what shine."

"Will what I have given away -- love, advice, be returned? I know that sounds selfish, but I feel so tired and stepped upon."

"You sound like every housewife I have sat on beds of throughout time."

I say, "That is dreadful. I am not a homemaker. I am hardly ever at home. I wish I were more. I have so much to do at home. Everything is out of its place, as you say. Do you think everything might move of itself into place? Of course not. I get exhausted thinking about it."

Gnome says, "Then, before you go to find where it all needs to go, picture it first. Picture its place. You may find things have plans you never dreamed of. So much is unorganized because you need to take the initiative, no one else will, to move the objects. They will speak their place if you think on them before you go to tidy up. Which, by the way, you need to do pretty soon, for I cannot stand to be in your clutter.

Tonight, I ask the cat to tell the Gnomes to come to a party. She blinks – as if she receives from my image of the picture of the party. She may not understand everything I say, but she sees the visual image.

I will try to play music for Gnome and Little Gnome. Other gnomes I have not met before are peering in the windows. Once, when I was quite young, I carried a flute with me at all times. I had stood in a large field on top a stone wall. As I played the music, a vast population of little people crowded into the field. They listened to me, and I said to them there, that I welcomed them, and I would always be their friend.

Although I don't mention Little Gnome often, I realized he was learning from Gnome about the human kingdom, and someday he would be able to speak to me.

The music I play is light and rhythmical. I picture my mother as a young woman dancing; for she is with me in thought. She and the gnome dance. She loves this moment. He laughs and kicks out his legs. It seems to last forever, but it is only a few minutes because I am home over my lunch break from work and playing the piano. Before I leave, I make a tea party for the gnomes, and my mother.

Even though I wanted a larger party, I think it must have felt long as eternity feels in that moment of the dance with the gnome. Many gnomes, I'd never met, looking in through the windows, the cats staring at us from the chairs – everyone was there after all. For, merriment had come into the room and warmth in my heart.

It rains with snow banked under trees. The woods are loud with peepers at night. They sing in wet places, beside ponds. They sing from dusk into the early morning.

The cats run in the shadows and the big dipper stands upright. The forest has a low wind. Grass is long. Crocuses emerge in the front beds, sticking out of snow. I walk through my garden, looking at stones. Winter turns them over. The quartz rock speaks, asking me to share my burdens.

I tell it about two burdens that I have. It absorbs my thoughts. You wouldn't think even small stones they are like sponges, but they are.

The wind is cold which will keep the crocuses lasting forever and the apricot buds will be in slow progression. On the long night before spring, there is an intense blackness of sky and stars are dim. The long wait for the snow to melt in the northern forest reminds me of my impatience to give birth after a long pregnancy, and the frustration of working at a job I wished to leave, but couldn't find a way out. You just have to wait.

Spring melts snow and the water dissolves into the soil, making it ready for planting.

As spring progresses, peepers shriek, making whistling sounds. They answer each other. Their calls make me want to walk all night in the woods.

The window is open. On my bed stand is a pile of books. There is one about old New York City in the early 20th century. Not so long ago I could easily read theses stories of the city. Now, even thinking about it after 9/11 is painful.

I used to go up to the roof of my aunt's apartment building in New York and watch the East River with the boats. I stood on tiptoe, and she'd tightly hold me. Then I listened to what was music to me: the slow rolling traffic honking, screeching below me. Constant horns of yellow taxicabs blared, as they wove through traffic jams. We'd take the elevator down to ground floor, go out into the street and shop at the corner grocery store. Just blocks away from this store the Twin Towers had fallen. It is my daughter Polly's birthday and I think of her all day, out in the Colorado Rockies. She loves the snow, skiing, being away right now from the east coast.

Waiting for spring involves leaving conflicts. The sadness is still with us all, especially at work. A nation's loss seems always mirrored with the personal, and the two tear apart. Which one takes priority? Which loss makes you feel guilty that you aren't mourning the other?

After we return to work after 9/11, we get to talking. They changed our shifts. People work mornings instead of evenings. In this mix up, we have the chance to share stories with people we have never sat beside. Why the mix up? People who sell well are pulled out of nights, put into day shifts. People, who are good at sympathy, are placed to deal with customers at night, after work hours.

I sit next to a new person who lost someone in the events of 9/11. Meanwhile I had recently heard from schoolmates, that my grade school teacher's daughter lost her husband in the second tower that fell. Finally, I have a personal story to share with co-workers. We feel a communal bond of being able to identify with people in New York City, once we had found our own stories.

I had known my teacher's family, having lived near them, and his daughter, although younger than I, had driven back and forth from school in a car with others and me each day. She was a quiet, sweet person; she became a nurse. I wondered how she managed to breathe even, with her husband gone like this. They had a five-year-old daughter who kept asking when her daddy was coming home. Amy had missed her husband's cell phone call minutes before the second tower collapsed. She had turned it off to tend to a patient.

If we appear sad about New York, our managers exclaim our sadness interacts with our sales, so they bark out – sell! sell! In addition, shout -- get over it, get on with work! –

I ask myself, Get over 9/11?

Yes, they rationalize it this way. We are 350 miles away. Don't let our emotions take over. Don't let hysteria collapse business.

Yet, when you constantly have to call New York City, as we do, no one there is over the tragedy and no one wants to talk with us unless we listen to his or her sadness. It takes a long time 'to get over' tragedy. How can corporate America bark out, get over it?

Loss not only mirrors other current losses, but brings back memories. My maternal grandmother lost her younger brother and sisters to scarlet fever and her father to tuberculosis. My miscarriage of a fifth child, when I was glad, but feeling guilty that I had been relieved of the burden of an unexpected pregnancy. Yet, I had dreams of this baby coming. I believe in reincarnation, so I think a baby will come back, but not to the situation, it intended. I am just one of the many it visited: the wind of a spring smile.

I wonder about Gnome. He is silent. Do troubled times affect a realm of our imagination, and keep the gnomes from entering thoughts?

There isn't a day we don't hear, or watch the news of war, terrorism, violence. The events of September slip into an unprocessed past of our national consciousness, and personal loss of how to understand the catastrophe except on terms of the poor economy which was already heading down hill before 9/11. The weather blows a greater storm in, and we have yet to see the clouds lift.

Gnome comes in and stands by the open window. Night air is fresh.

He says, "This year is as a mirror fractured slightly. You notice a difference, but you still know the reflection shines. Over time, the real image replaces the mirror. A curtain now falls across our elemental world to shield us from violence and the chaos that the atmosphere around your world has been in."

He continues, "Remember your own visualizations. In this time where you wait for more to come, for my visits, remember the journeying that I taught you to take, the departing from a place and returning to it. Travel to your intentions and ideals, and then focus on the point of return. This point is your landing again on earth. The vanishing point in a painting is the point of return.

"Don't leave off the journeying in your imagination. Trust the sea, the wind and the air to carry you to places where you can dwell for a while and regain inspiration. Spend a few moments and you will feel it is a lifetime you have traveled."

Gnome had told me to see into the light, feel it as breath, and feel it going into me through my eyes and skin and smile and the release from myself the dark light, night out into the fresh morning. The light throbs around us and we can feel the joy of it as winds. I received also another thought, but forgot it and I did not write it down.

A chair, pillows, stools —these are objects to have in a room for the gnomes. A small stool is for the little gnome, so his feet can touch the floor. Pillows are on the floor if they want to sit low.

"Play music." Gnome stands by my desk.

"I haven't been able to play music."

"Music is part of you. You will make yourself happy to play it. Why is it so hard to do?"

I look at the papers on my desk.

He says, "I don't understand. It is easy to play, yet hard to get to the place of playing it. Take it out of the case -- decide on a song to play. The effort is huge."

"I don't know why it is hard to play," I reply.

"It is too easy for you, that is why. You are seeking for things which are at a distance.. You think things should be hard, but the challenge is taking the instrument from its case, and you can't surmount even this simple task. Be honest. Now play music." he commands.

Gnome leaves. I put down this journal, and try to forget what he said. Despite his sudden impatience with me, I can't play music just because he commands it.

The garden herbs rise out of the soil. Some of them had a tough winter. I forgot to cover the lemon balm in autumn leaves for the winter. The leaves are slow to come out on the bushes because of this neglect. Spring is here. The grass gets thicker. Snow is in the forest, but not anymore on the lawn. In my garden, I turn over stones while thinking about people. The job relationships in our corporate ladder are difficult. The managers who are right above us, act arrogant, and lesser human beings. The phone customers, depending on the kind of jobs they have, are also jerks. They are the ones that linger in my mind after the workday is over, or after a phone call is finished. Why do people stick in one's thoughts after work?

Gnome sits in the woods, maybe listening to my thoughts. As he walks closer, I see he wears green velvet trousers. Maybe he knows I like green velvet. Like I said, my aunt, an artist, used to say that the little people knew what you liked, and wore for you what you wanted to see them dressed in. Her gnomes wore berets, and carried art pads and pencils with them when they appeared to her because she loved art.

Gnome says, "When you feel distant from somebody, picture their eyes. Go into their eyes and dwell there, feel how it is to be in their eyes. You will find that each face, each set of eyes looks different, that is, from within. You can find them very simply by wishing to reach the person. The fastest way to reach someone at any moment is to go into their soul via the door of the eyes."

I begged Gnome and Little Gnome to come to my daughter's June wedding. Reflecting on this, now, I watch how the morning slithers through the eastern forest. Green, a color of harmony, blends with trees and fields. Gray fog lifts from the mountains. Day begins.

My daughter's wedding was a few days ago. It lifts in memory. It was a short marriage – two years? -- I think back on the events, wedding guests. Her quiet face, and soft bridal gown, the bridesmaids' excited faces. A wedding speaks about the beauty of the young, the wisdom of the carved faces of the old. I want to remember how the spring flowers bloomed and the sea waves crashed, and in her outdoors wedding, here in the north, it was a long spring. The low tide turned with a sigh, the wedding guests sighed. I did not feel good about this wedding and I couldn't say why.

I asked the gnomes to come with me to the ceremony. With them there, I could relax because the atmosphere changed, and other beings popped out of bushes, stone walls, and trees to also be present at the wedding. The gnomes' presence there made me trust that whatever may come of this marriage, our daughter was protected, for they were watching over her.

During the music at the wedding, the gnomes sat on the bench, tapping their feet to the rhythm. The violinist was extremely skilled, and at ease with his playing, smiling even when he played the hardest passages. The gnomes were dressed perfectly for the event. They wore deep purple velvet suits, and white, laced shirts. They were intent on two things: my daughter and the music. The bridegroom was so worried looking, that he gave little pleasure to them, I thought.

As I mingled afterwards with everyone, attended the reception, I lost concentration on the gnomes, and they disappeared.

Summer 2002

By the sea, ospreys fly, seals bark in a cove, a young bald eagle screams from its nest in a fir tree on a close small island.

Funny how it is when you want to make a conversation with someone and you wish you weren't alone, than presto, someone is there and you think how on earth you didn't realize that person was there all the time. It is like thinking of someone you love who has died. Then, it seems suddenly, they walk with you, and they've been beside you without you knowing it.

The tide is low, and the shore reveals its life: sand dollars, crab shells, several species of sea weeds. I watch the gulls and terns and wonder how the beauty around me could be so real this day and how I have such privilege of being alive and on this beach.

Gnome and Little Gnome are behind me. When I stop walking and let them catch up, I say "Hey, nice seeing you out here. I didn't know you'd come with me out here to this island."

I wondered what conversation of nature and human beings interacting would take place today. Tramping this beach, alone, feeling refreshed from the sea air, I'm not too keen on talking. The other day, gnome asked me to reflect on the element of moisture. Of rain, of snow, of the melting of winter. Of the spring's growth in its unfolding and blossoming, and freshness and life lasting far into summer. Living into the element of moisture was not like living in the element of air -- air gave me wings, inspiration, flight. Air was above the earth, it felt good to be in air.

Moisture felt heavy, dense and slow to move. Sometime it felt good, other times it felt as if my skin and body had no boundary with the leaves and grass and bushes, and trees.

On the beach, the water is cold. The gnomes keep on their leather boots.

"Every intricate thing you see is mystery," Gnome emphasizes, as we walk.

The sweep of sea and landscape, with its fir trees, rocks, distant islands is about the wholeness of each detail.

"It is sensing the detail, not always seeing it. Vastness has infinite parts, each one reliant on another part -- you look at the sea--- what do you see?"

We approach large rocks. Low tide leaves pools in crevices of rocks. On the side of the rocks many limpet shells cling. Each shell is a living creature, dependent on the tides; they digest part of this sea's organisms for food. The sea spreads seaweed on the sand-- some of it as fine as moss.

How did the world form this beauty? What variations of detail did a greater Mind imagine for the universe? These questions drift out sea. The gnomes leave without me noticing.

When I return home from the island, I go to my herb garden. I need time to transition between the two landscapes: sea and forested inland. Gardens are for me a place to hide behind plants, where I can think. The sea is restful, of dreams. I don't work by the sea, I rest. In a garden is work to keep the borders clear, the plants health.

The island gives you fresh ideas. I watch the currents as I row a boat into different coves.

In the herb garden the melted snow makes the soil rich. Lemon balm and sage burst from stone border.

I ask the Gnome what is the point of sensing the detail of each thing, being within each form?

Gnome says, "You will increase your own power when you work with matter in this way. Picture the detail of nature as strongly as you can. Be within everything in your garden."

I pull out some weeds from the lemon balm and spend the afternoon wheeling dead leaves away to the woods. That evening, I run a bath. Black flies bit, and dried blood is caked on my neck.

Gnome peers in the door, "Picture someone you have had a painful relationship with. Put them into a picture of detail. Paint the surroundings of this person. When they hurt you, recall this picture you have made of them in a place." Now he is on the bathroom stool, kicking his legs.

I tell him it might not be proper for him to be talking to me as I take my bath.

He says, "My world is not proper. The way I am seeing you is not the way you humans see each other. Let's leave it at that." Nonetheless, he turns away from the shower curtain, to face the wall.

I ease into the water, closing the shower curtain away from him. As my mind relaxes, I begin to picture several people. I put each person separately into a detailed picture where I encountered them, remembering the place very clearly.

"Do you see this in your mind?" he calls.

"Yes."

"Say what you feel."

"I wish I'd done this before. The picture surrounding the person tells you about the person. I would have saved myself time and painful experiences had I known the effects of meditating like this on a person."

I had tried for many years to make these several relationships right and now it seemed in vain. I couldn't change someone else, no matter how I felt for the good of that person, they needed to make their own changes themselves. I had to step back, and be patient, and never think I had the solution, just the picture of the person, the infinite image of what the Creator must feel toward creation.

"In that picture," he adds, "you can place and hear the detail of a person. Picture it as closely as you can, see the pattern of the picture, even in very infinite detail. You will know how to approach the person."

He walks around the bathroom, "If there is no likeness to the detail, then, for you, it is best to give a wide space for the person, respect his space, know you can't change their imperfection -- it is cast for this lifetime. It is their fate, if that is what you say. You will know if you have made an error -- it will be like a lone figure you have created, wandering about."

I ask gnome, "What of moisture, then-- how does water help us?"

He answers," To visualize yourself within water, allows you the focus of staying within a thought, a project, a study, the process of completion, of coming to grips with a job, any work, effort. Get into it, feel the element of moisture -- you are in a bath now -- outside, you can be within rain, stream waters flowing, visualize water if you aren't near it -- remember to observe your feelings as you do when you take a walk, look at objects in your garden, stones, flowers. Be patient and work with care and concern for nature and people."

When I start to think, and explore what he has told me, he slips away – as he does now-- and the space around me is empty again. I get out of my bath, dress, and go to bed.

The gnome, having told me so many times to observe detail in nature, asks me now to observe everything in a peripheral sphere. What exists in a circle around me to acknowledge it and bring it into my awareness; especially in the beauty of summer to be aware of spatial forms and to feel myself a part of these forms: of leaf, bud, tree, plant, animal.

This brings quietness. The fear of terrorists, economic downfall makes despair enter the work day, because now there is fear not having jobs.

"Look on everything, every detail-- smells, colors," Gnome reiterates continually when I am close to fright. Sitting by a flower, observing it closely, smelling the roses at the border of the garden, calms me.

The summer is not too dry, nor wet. The colors are strong; in berries, which we have been picking, is deep purple, which is grounding for the soul

Autumn comes early; summer still is in the process of completion. The garden is producing and more fruits are ripening. The air is crisp; tops of trees turn colors, but summer wants to linger.

I beg the gnome to be present. I am feeling out of touch with myself. When he is with me, then I no longer feel empty. His world, in which so many invisible elements exist alongside ours, is a soothing balm.

Gnome stands at the corner of the garden, by the bee balm herbs. These are bright red plants, which attract bees and give off a strong, lovely odor. He sees me sitting on the grass, and must realize how exhausted I am because he talks about how I can visualize energy. It is simpler than I think, because it is right in front of me. He says, "Look at vertical objects -- everything that is height, and low, live into that force and energy. This is not intellectual, just blend into this force."

He disappears, and I walk on the garden path, and look up into the birch tree. Its white branches move in the stillness of the day. There is wind up there, I say to myself, even though I cannot see it, the branches stir. I sit on a stone, imagining this wind vitalizing me.

On another autumnal morning while walking to work, I sense footsteps beside me. The big and little Gnomes catch up to me.

Birds sharply call as they prepare to leave the north. Sometimes you can nearly understand what they are saying. I had an experience in a garden where I worked years ago when I heard the words of the birds. I was shocked to be able to understand their language. In that garden, closed in on all four sides by hedges, I sat back from weeding, and looked up to the tall ash trees, watching the birds flit from branch to branch, calling ordinary things. Hurry up, stop quarreling, and wait for me. It was not profound speech, but simple.

One of my daughters understood chickens clucking when she was young. I think it is like hearing a foreign language. At first, you cannot get a word, but if you hear it long enough, the babble becomes comprehendible. Isn't this what happened in the story of the Tower of Babel? Magic happened.

Here, as I garden, Gnome says, "Imagine how chickens who converse in their own language feel to be caged up, and killed for food. Do you people realize how intimate, conversational fowl and beast are?"

"Do you eat meat?"

Gnome shakes his head. "We are in a sphere beyond the physical. You will be in a similar space when you die. You consume on your earth what you need. But when you consume it think on the spirit of the animal, and its life."

On these August mornings, as I listen to the birds, remembering the garden in which I had understood them, I am sad that I can no longer. Maybe gifts come for just a moment -- you cannot make them last. Winds take them on for somebody else.

Early Winter 2002

Snow falls. Winter is early. The woodstove blazes. Gnomes and cats spread out on rugs. One of the cats, the youngest, licks her paws and now moves to the underneath part of the stove.

The stove hisses and flames rise and die back to embers. You have to stoke the stoves well for the night. In early morning, someone gets up early to feed it.

You keep a rhythm with the seasons. Winter requires warmth. Fires burn in stoves, smoke rises out of chimneys. The village looks like an old fashioned, timeless world of clapboard homes, smoke, and forest looming beyond. It doesn't seem that time hasn't changed here too much. The sound missing is the clip-clop of horses' hooves, their neighs.

Brittle, cracking sounds of the trees pierce the northern night. Wind creaks the firs, and you stay inside. In the morning, I'll go out in the woods on skis and follow tracks along the streams. You ski through woods and feel like moose must do, just going off trails into the brush.

A man stopped my son in these back woods and said he had bought the land. "Get off," he said. My son replied, "Sir, I have been walking these woods since a child and you are telling me to get out of them?" "Yes," he replied and threatened prosecution for trespassing. He set up cameras in the trees to catch trespassers. The woods and neighbors are changing here. We joke it is Homeland Security.

The Gnome says, "You can't be invisible and walk as we, through the woods unseen by most people – this is a shame. We are happy to be invisible and we can avoid the issue of trespassing. How strange that is. Do you know how many unseen things pass through your world?"

"Am I offensive because I trespass in your world?" he asks. I say no, but if people could see all the spirits, certainly they would try to prosecute them all for dwelling in what we think of as private homes and woods.

He replies, "A home is a house of spirits. The more one can accept that, the easier it is to let it be. You bump into the other world constantly and never know it."

With the snow, comes a sense of peace. There is nothing like it. You put the world away -- the room gets warm, the woodstove hums. It is said that this contentment is the earthly experience of another world, of Devachan. The Swedenborgs speak in terms of associations. What is in Heaven, has an associative symbol on earth. A sense of peace on earth, lives on in Heaven.

Every autumn, you wonder if you've put enough wood away for winter. Each year you worry, yet something usually turns up to alleviate these fears. Maybe, it is a friend saying: I know someone who has dry, cheap cord wood. If it's not dry, you don't say no. You put in the back of the barn keeping it for April burning.

On long nights, when fears stare in the windows, Gnome says, "When one lives deeply into each day, listening to it, the next one follows logically, in sequence of the previous day. This way, everything will work out in its own time."

The cat gets up from under the stove. She sees my pen moving and bats at it. I observe her symmetrical markings. How the M between her eyes formed so perfectly. How as she ages, her eyelashes cover her eyes. She is a tiny cat, found as a kitten in the woods beneath a mountain, in the middle of nowhere. She was three weeks old, and the hunter gave her to my son who brought her home and she fit into the palm of my hand. She slept under my neck at night, and wandered about my garden in the day, hiding underneath the comfrey leaves.

She knows me well enough. I didn't used to be a cat person, but I have gotten to like them because my husband won't have dogs. Her sensing is intuitive, unspoken, but communicative to me. She looks long into objects, as if she and the Gnome are teachers, asking me to take notes of how to be present in a moment.

When she was a kitten, as soon as she could follow me, we explored the woods. She learned to grip on to the trunks, leap across brooks. She cried when she needed carrying. Through each season, she grew. She walked through snow and on top of ice. When her paws got cold, I carried her inside my jacket or in the side pocket where she could stick out her head.

We stopped to look at birds or an animal track. We watched spring snow recede and plants rise from the last year's autumn leafed floor.

Sometimes I felt I looked through her eyes into the woods. Movements and unseen forms and noises seemed close. A leaf broke from the tree, fell into the brook, got carried by the current downstream, until it was trapped in an eddy, swirled under a rock.

Now here, indoors, you feel between outdoor and inside, longing for the harmony of both to be within. It takes a while to settle into winter. There's an in between time that has to happen, between leaving behind the green woods and entering the season of ice.

Gnome goes all over the woods in summer – it is easy to do. As winter comes in, I have to wait to catch a glimpse of him, perhaps, sitting on the kitchen table and kicking his legs.

I remember how he tells me to live into things. Be patient. Slow down. Observe the ordinary things. The dustpan at angles to the stove, its brush several feet away like a disconnected thought. A pair of boots by the dust brush as if they will walk away, for they, too, are not part of a conscious thought.

The cat begins to play, running under the rug, and then lies on it, displaying her white fur of her stomach. She looks at me as if to say, are you going to play?

When I am sad, the Gnome says, "Play music."

Music sweeps through a room as fresh mountain air, but I still can't force myself to make the music.

The cat wants to play and slides under the rug, then pounces on it. As I sit by the stove, the cat returns to watch the pencil. Her head moves as my hand moves and she jumps up to my paper to sit on it.

If Gnome comes, I'll make a cup of tea, put out shortbread, and relax. Outside, the snow blows. I'll walk to work next morning with a ski pole. As I get out the shortbread, Gnome appears.

"To have inspiration to make music and to walk to work in the bitter cold, you must use imagination. Picture warmth around you, a gold color, everywhere you walk."

I thank him. It is important to thank a gnome for helping.

I'll work on imagination of a scene that I realize is not only physical, but perfectly possible to visualize and create the gold color and warmth around me.

Gnome sits on a cushion on the floor. I say, "I am going to bed. You can find a place by the stove to sleep -- it is so cold outside, and be welcome in our house." I do not know where the Gnome sleeps outside. It could be in a tree stump or log in the forest. It could be somewhere in his Invisible dimension where it is not cold.

Sometimes the Gnome wants to talk with me after I've left the room. That does happen. Like yesterday, as I was about to get in my bath, he appeared and I said, "You can't come in this time, very sorry."

"Alright," he said, and sat outside the door.

I wanted no distractions and no conversation. A bath on a cold winter night takes away worry.

It takes time for Gnome to reappear. It serves me right for not wishing to speak with him when I took that bath and told him not to come in. I only wished to lie back and forget my world. To cast off the workday, the pressure put on us to sell products we don't like. What else to do in the hinterlands of forests, lakes and howling winds, where winter is longer than summer?

Jobs are gone before you can apply for them and there is a certain amount of nepotism that takes place in an isolated area, where if you are the cousin of a good worker, or the son, or aunt, you have more of a chance to get work. In my job, I knew someone who got me in. We are paid slightly more than people who work at McDonalds, but it is severely stressing if you can't get fired up to sell over the telephone something you'd never take yourself.

When I am frustrated, I can't put myself into Gnome's space. I do not understand dimensions, in the sense of physics, but I only know that they are there. I can't rationally explain them, but that doesn't mean they don't exist. We are hardly able to see what is in front of us on our physical plane. The dreaming I go into for these conversations, is part of another real space.

Gnome returns. He says, "Look, here I am sitting at the end of your bed!"

I say, "And still kicking your legs."

"Yes."

Little Gnome, who hides behind the bed, peeks out; his cap falls off his head.

Gnome shakes his hat, winks and reiterates, "Live into everything completely. Each person, each event, each thing that confronts you. Don't think about it, judge it, solve it, Just be in it." This is his teaching – the same old stuff, like a professor going over a simple algebraic equation again and again.

I say goodnight and I turn off my light.

Other times, Gnome says, "Be with the animals."

How can I be with animals, when my house is full of people. My son is home with his college friends, and I am wishing to be alone. At times I felt bombarded with the past, and all that I wished I could do for the holidays, but can't seem to organize. I compare myself to my mother and grandmother, all who had parties, and decorations, and beautiful things displayed to uplift one in this season. There are longings in me and disappointments and now the criticism the children throw at me of my imperfections. They want those kind of things at this time of year. I like to be quiet, and sit in front of the lit tree, and reflect on the year. This season is one of seeking inner peace. The things that accompany this festive holiday are nonsense to me and I have no passion for the colored lights, decorations, cakes, food. What I picture are goblets of heavy glass and velvet curtains on windows. And fires in fireplaces that we don't have -- we just have a woodstove. And long tables in front of the fire places. People mingling with each other in mellow conversations. That is my idea of this season. Candle lights, gnomes all around, but invisible.

Gnome doesn't say more than a sentence to me. A helpful piece of advice, to make me stop, think and say, what do you mean?

When a house is over populated, there seems to be one person needed to be on duty the whole time. No one sees everything that person does, only the place would be a mess if the invisible hands to wash the dishes, dry them put them away, seep the floors, cook were not there. It is I. I am sure of this role I fall into and then wonder if I have any other role. I get swamped quickly and can hardly hear my own thoughts nor do they seem to matter. Plus, there's also more I am not saying, I hardly say it to myself.

I was nearly ready to quit this role, catch a flight to someplace else in the world, where I could be me, alone, I dreamed of running to an Indian woman called Amma Chi who hugs everyone. She might just hug me, and that is all I need. In the swirl of these thoughts, I looked out of my eyes and saw Gnome. I said, help.

Gnome, in the midst of my disorderly home, points to the cats asleep under the stove.

"Look at them."

I pat them, brush them, feed them more food, get a string and play with them. They are very much with me, and I have deep peace and serenity.

He sits on my study bed. Outside, the moon is disappearing below the forest. A cloud comes over and dims it. The sky is brilliantly sparkling. We have little snow this winter. The air is dry. I took a walk tonight and could hear the wind, making the trees groan and creak and my boots creaked, too, as I walked the snow- covered streets. No one was out. I was walking off my mood rather than cast if on my family, which I did I am afraid, so I left then to get it out of my system.

Gnome says, "You are waiting."

"For what?"

"To throw the stone in another direction and follow it and where it lands is exactly how you have to be, casting out your ideas, doing them, not knowing where they will land."

I lean on the desk and gaze outside at the snow. The moon makes shadows on the ground, and lightens clouds. It is a night if one dresses warmly, to walk, but I have done this already, and I am ready to sleep. Sleep brings forgetting. Sleep remembers the day in new images where we wander away from earth through the night.

I put away my workday and wander downstairs, not out into the night, but to warm up by the stove. Gnome lingers before leaving me. I tell him I like how he is dressed tonight. He wears a fur coat, hat, and boots, which look Scandinavian. They are made of thick fur, with pointed toes, red tassels, and bells hang from them. He jingles as he walks. He waves. "Dress up! Go downtown! Watch a movie! Drink coffee in the café!"

He goes out the door, disappearing like the snow blowing up into the trees.

I dream I get into the boat and return to the city and climb the stairs. Gnome comes with me. He asks, "Finally you return. Why – what is the reason for being away from this journeying?"

"I had to get back confidence, that I wasn't crazy doing this."

Gnome walks into the large room. A person sits at the desk.

Gnome asks, "Well, are you going to just gape at her? What is the matter?"

"I freeze."

He says, "You take this journey, and then you arrive here, but you only look at the editors at their desks and don't know what to do."

I say, "I wanted it to be different this time. I'd go up to a desk and a different person who is cheerful, warm and friendly. Someone I feel drawn to."

He asks, "What significance is warmth to you?"

"I feel creative with warmth around me. I guess – when someone is trying to help, the warmth of heart is like a flowing stream."

January, 2003

Wind chill factors are far below zero. The house is full of drafts. High ceilings lift the warm air upwards. The only way to stay warm is to sit near the wood stove. Once, each room must have had a stove. Then, over a century ago, many cords of wood were burned each winter. In a big house, you usually burn six to eight cords. Long ago before oil, people who lived in this house easily burned sixteen. Wood was abundant. Now, oil is not cheap. Wood is costly, unless you own a part of the forest. You have to look for ways of not burning oil.

Gnome is close to the fire. I ask him.

"Where will you sleep tonight?"

He shrugs, "By the stove in a corner." He points to the woodpile close to the stove. "We will watch the stove."

I ask, "How do you sleep?"

"Sometimes not at all. We look around us, especially at the cats and mice, and many more things."

"Do you mind telling me what many other things you see in our house at night?"

Gnome shakes his head. "No. It will frighten you and others. A house is full of many wandering, departing coming and going -- spirits. We call them thoughts."

I ask, "What are they like?"

Gnome answers, "Wisps of air, sometimes. Or clouds, masses of heaviness, roaming, moving."

I ask, "Like, the cats and mice you watch?"

"Yes, especially the mice. They are carriers of matter, and dart into such places as you or I never can go. They go into dark places and move things around in them."

I ask, "What do you mean?"

He says, "The dark space would be dead air, almost solid, not moving. These small creatures come into the dark crevices and nooks of especially old homes and stir the dark, hidden air. They see, you do not."

"So, the Universe has a reason for every creature, more than what we think of, say, a mouse, as?"

"Of course." The gnome blinks, then vanishes.

The study has a fold up seat, made of a canvas -- an art chair my aunts used in the 1930's through the 1960's when they sat outdoors in front of their easels to paint. You folded it up, carried it off then. It is wooden. Not one stitch of plastic, of course. It was a heavier, solid world, no chemical aura around. Don't you feel it when you have a plastic object in the room? Something leaves the room with plastic. Something unreal enters.

Plastic they say, emits a chemical vapor. Within 18 inches of a plastic object, one is in contact with this substance. It is a real vapor. You could picture it like something shining with white small worms slithering about. The substance is sticky and attaches itself to you and it goes into your body - presto.

Gnome comes into the study.

"You are thinking of the negative stuff. Pollution that jams up the earth, makes your people ill."

His eyes flash. I think, he wants to ban talk about this kind of negative stuff and plastics tonight.

I say, "I read news articles which say to take away most everything used in the home, made of plastic. Also, banish the chemical cleaners – the ones in my bathroom closet—go back to basics -- vinegar, soda, which is also in the closet. Use cloth bags for bagging and cheesecloth for wrapping an item in the refrigerator."

He gets up and paces the room. "You mustn't go into details of negatives. Stop talking. Think on better things."

He looks at the walls with photographs of my family on them. He sees the paintings. I am reading books, drinking tea. I walk home at night watching the stars. Each day the light returns more strongly and lasts longer. It used to be I would step out of work in pitch dark at 4:30 p.m. and watch these stars constantly as I went up hill to our house, going through the University campus, through the streets of town, along the dark fir trees.

It is -15 degrees F. and 13 degrees by day. It is so cold that I think back on how it was when I was young and heard stories of the north woods and never dreamed I would come north to live.

It was said winter drove you crazy. The snow never left until spring. The cold grew icicles on your face.

I feel a familiar tug on my sleeve. Gnome is wrapped in a wool scarf and a dark soft green vest and a purple - maroon knit hat. He wears knitted gloves, brown wool trousers and leather boots with fur inside. He kicks his feet - as usual – as he sits on the table.

"How are you?"

"Do you know how hard it is to work in a corporation? The last two years have been hell."

He gets down from the table and sits on a chair.

I continue, "You have come with me to work sometimes, haven't you?"

He begins to fade away. Maybe he doesn't want to answer this.

If he speaks right now, I cannot hear his words. Perhaps, there are no words. My focus left me, as I wander into another room, not caring to talk at him, when he has nothing to say.

Sitting in this tiny study, I sense Mabel by me. Looking out the window, down to the street below me, I watch the shifts of nurses come to the nursing home, which is opposite my house. I feel as if Mabel makes me think thoughts. I think about my neighbors, wondering how their day went. Tonight, I am thinking in dollar bills. It is my job at work, money, so it comes sneaking up on my thoughts when I come home. I see one house roof, and I take a guess how much they make. I see another steep, gabled roof with an old chimney and estimate their income. I go down and up the street. I come to my own roof, which is tin over wooden shingles, steep, angles, many roofs on this old home. My husband is without a job, but at least, I have work. My aunt left me money, but I have had to use it all. I estimate the different incomes we make on this street, and I think what if we pooled all this together and did a much different life style. Your mortgage, rent, home expenses, including oil and wood bills, health care needs are this and that – so out of the pooled money you can take what is needed. There will always be enough there in this pool.

No – it would not work. The larger income of the doctor at the end of the street, in the mansion, keeps us from knowing him casually. It shouldn't, but it does. It is only my mind that creates this barrier. I must work on the possibility of knowing someone apart from their life style.

I see smoke rising from chimneys. We have a necessity in common. We must keep warm. Icicles, which hang seven feet in length from each roof, reflect the street lamps' lights. Behind our homes, are dark woods, called the Northern Woods, where one can get on a trail and cross into Canada, and continue to Labrador. In these woods are the coyotes, the bobcats, the bears, foxes, deer, moose.

A phone call came today that a priest I had known for years, died. Gnome is close to the telephone, he looks like he wants to touch it. I hold it like a stone, at a distance from me; it almost drops on the floor. I recall many talks with her over the years. Then, I think of Mabel. She didn't know this woman, but suddenly she and the priest seem close to me in my room. They stand beside the gnome.

Gnome looks from the telephone to these women. He has been knitting a sock.

He whispers to me, "Look, you need to master this grief. You don't need to grieve her passing like you did Mabel's."

I felt he was being harsh with me. I looked startled, I guess.

He says, "There are people who just take grief and hold on to it. Some grief is very important, but you can decide for yourself. This woman had a role in your life, she was a priest, not a friend to you, remember this."

I shift in my chair. He is right. I have to let this go.

He goes on, "Recall your memories of the priest, and picture each detail of, say, one memory of her. Think on this tonight. When this fades, bring up another memory. Keep doing this until you can let go of her a bit – until the next wave of sadness comes over you."

A week after 9/11, this priest had listened to my description of Mabel's death, and then we had spoken about the terrorists attack. And now, my priest friend, unexpectedly, has departed. She had a very short bout with cancer. She left gracefully, with most of her larger network of friends not knowing the few months of her intense suffering. She told few except very close friends of her cancer.

Tonight memories shift the forms of these two women. Perhaps they feel my thoughts going out to them. Mabel is smiling at me. With my priest friend, it isn't so close as that. Although she'd come into my room, she now stands on a hill, looking down at the landscape. She has reserve and distance in her viewing of the world she left.

Gnome says, "In her lifetime, your priest tried to have conversations with us."

I remember how she used to speak to me about an elemental world of another dimension, but I didn't know if she actually saw it. She spoke as if I didn't know it. And this had made me silent. I never like this attitude, that the person in front of you isn't a person who has some close beliefs and similar experiences or, something to say. This is one of my problems with priests. It would have been the same attitude if she'd been talking about God.

For those who can't see inwardly, one can sense the gnome world, which is perhaps, almost as good as seeing it. Reading folk tales, even modern day tales, like the stories of the Swedish painter, John Bauer, and the Norwegian stories of the D'Aulaire's, helps to imagine this other mysterious world.

They say death comes in threes. Next, a theater friend and father in law of Mabel's daughter, died. We crossed on a ferry to a very small island where he lived with his family. On this day I had disembarked from the ferry, finding my own way there, not knowing that a car was waiting for us.

We packed into an old hostel, which overlooks the sea. Many of his college students had come to this memorial to recollect together his classes, because he had inspired many of them to do things in their lives they might not have done without his encouragement.

After the memorial, there was a procession of drums, pipes and trumpets. It lead us to his yard beside the sea and to a fruit tree where he wanted his ashes buried. His wife placed them into the ground. His son covered them. The ocean waves crashed.

Although I had only met him at Mabel's and didn't know him or his wife in any other setting, I was told he had always invited friends to visit them on this island. It is three miles in circumference. The dirt road around it is not used very much. People walk on small lanes, in between the houses where the sea wind doesn't blow too hard. Someone played a violin.

Perhaps, a reason for holding a celebration of a person's life, is meeting those who knew the departed in different times, places, years. It brings together as a circle, that person's life.

There are island people there, too. The hostel's living room holds everyone. Downstairs on the ground floor is the large kitchen, with many gas stoves and tin sinks. On the top floor, are sparsely furnished bedrooms, with braided rugs and white walls. Sea wind blows through each window.

Reflecting on the day, I think the Gnome was with me, only I didn't notice.

I ask, "Were you there?"

Gnome replies, "I was there."

The hostel was cold. There was no heating. I had heard someone say they wouldn't be able to sleep with it being so cold. I told the person a story about Dylan Thomas, the poet....

what you do, I said, is to shake out the rug on the floor, put it on top of you, on top of the covers, the way Dylan Thomas did. Dylan Thomas? someone said. Yeah, I said. He was known for putting rugs and even window curtains on top of himself at night for extra weight plus warmth to make him sleep. People stared at me as if I'd know him. What a detail to know about someone's life.

It is evening in my study.

"Are you cold?"

Gnome is hugging his knees as he rests in the chair.

He needs something. He seems downcast. I could dance an Irish jig for him.

He reads my thoughts. "No dancing tonight," he says.

I lift up my head and part the window curtains to look out – into the stars, into the past, when my grandmother jigged when she was sad or tired. I watched her feet tap the rhythm first, then she began to sing the music to jig with. Her eyes remained serious, but everything else about her became music, dance.

Gnome is quiet. He, too, seems reflective. I have gone back in memory where I border on loneliness, missing loved relatives. He seems to have something on his mind.

"You must have a picture now. Build up a picture around yourself."

I am confused. A picture?

He continues, "You are the painter. Imagine a painting around you. Get into it once you paint it. Try out different scenes, until you find the one you like best to be in."

"Is this real?" I ask.

Gnome says, "Well, what is real? You wake up each morning and you don't know how the day will be. It is entirely up to your vision of the day, how your day will be. your ideas, your imagination. You have to move into the day more wakefully, that is all. Painting pictures of landscapes and portraits of yourself is not easy, but you will find that they come more easily once you start exercising that which is called imagination."

"Is this why I have no inspiration anymore it seems?" I ask.

He replies, "You cannot rely on other people to create your picture. If other people want into your picture then let them be outside of it, looking at it."

The candle on my table is burning low. He looks at me with a soft gaze. As if he is fading into another world, seeing me at a distance.

"I am sorry to be so tired tonight," I say.

"You must hold water in a glass up to the sunshine in the daytime and say your own name and drink the water as an elixir."

He continues, "Your own name is a magic name, that gives you life. It is usually not the same name given you at birth by your family. Sometimes it is, but it is rare. The magic name is the name that you are given throughout all time, all eternity."

Watching the news -- there is an anti- war march going on in Washington, DC. It seems huge. As large as the first Woodstock? No way, I say. I remember being at Woodstock.

Gnome is suddenly beside me, as usual intercepting my thoughts.

"It's not large enough," he says.

"Not large enough?" I wonder.

"No," he insists."Many more people have to show their dissatisfaction with the possibility of war."

I was in Ireland just before the outbreak of the war there in the late 1960's. My family wanted me to go back to Ireland to meet the relatives and spend my junior year abroad at boarding school near Dublin. One of my classmates was afraid of the IRA in the streets at night, running up and down lanes, searching out people, children of people. She thought they'd get her. This country invents fear. I am not sure that Ireland did. Those men were real at night.

Gnome says, "The wind and rain and the sea and the snow will turn against this country if you don't face what is happening."

I ask, "War?"

"Yes. You know it is not a war on any ordinary level. Life will get very hard for your country," Gnome says.

"Do you travel outside this country?" I ask.

"Yes, when you don't see me, there are times when I am gone. I am traveling. I am okay, I am safe. I can tell you someday where all I go. It is very busy now. We must travel very fast."

Recently, I'd been standing at the ruins of 9/11. I had gone down with my son and his friends to see the Red Sox play the Yankees. I really wanted to see the site of the terrorist attacks. To remember how my uncle walked near the towers to work on Wall Street each day. He said to us children when we visited him and our aunt that he went to keep the wolf from the door each day. Now I was thinking about this great terrible wolf. My uncle died and he couldn't keep it away anymore. Now, this creature, fear, was lurking in the streets everywhere. He never knew the disaster that would come.

"Were you in NYC with me by the ruins?" I ask.

"Yes."

"I am sorry, I wasn't aware of you there."

"It is alright."

"Well, I was there. The rain was falling."

"Yeah, and it didn't matter how wet we all got. We all were staring at nothing. But everything. If I were a mother of someone lost there, I would not have been able to see this site."

"I know," he says.

We continue sitting on the sofa together as the light fades in the sky, and the year is about to end. He fades away, and I go to bed.

The cat lives in the cellar this winter. Spider webs hang on the stairs and rafters. They are worse in summer and fall than in winter, but still thick enough this month for me to have to use a broom, to clear the webs away to get down the stairs. The floor is dirt. The walls are thick, made of stone. With a small woodstove hooked up down here, and all the spiders cleared out, this space would be warm and special. It would be wonderful to be in an airtight place away from the winter winds, which blow through cracks in the windows and doors upstairs.

What torture we subject ourselves to, living in winter in the north. What expenses we pay to live in its white elegance. We could live underground in winter,with cramped quarters in a cellar, and not burn oil. There are many rooms in our house. It is far from practical to heat them all. We do, however, keep the minimum heat them so the pipes don't freeze. But in winter I'd rather be under the ground and warm.

Underground one can feel the earth. I know an artist near us, who lived in a hole in the ground with a woodstove in it and heavy canvas over the roof of the hole. The woodstove pipe came straight up and somehow the canvas didn't burn. Now he has a job as an artist in residence on cruise ships during the coldest months. He is earning money to start building a house above ground.

I am too tired tonight. The cold has been with us very long with no January thaw. For two weeks it has been – 10 degrees F. at night and tonight it will go down to – 40F.,which includes wind chill factor.

Two of my children have returned home. They have transferred degrees to our hometown's University. I am glad they are here, but I have to tell them to turn down the heat and they will find this difficult. Oil costs are rising. There is talk that there isn't enough oil left in the world.

Over the last few weeks, I noticed the cat kept coming up the stairs from the cellar, opening the door and staring at me. When I approached her, she ran down again. For many days this was the case. I open the door, looked at the cat, who looked back at me, then I closed the door. I left food and water for her on the top step.

She has a reason for asking me to come down with her. I stand still on the steps. I realize I am dismissing her action as strange, but nothing to follow up. On the kitchen table I'd placed my mittens and hat and bag, all ready for work. The teapot sits on the grill of the woodstove.

I think it is in moments when you are very present in a place then gaze out as it were into another space, let go for a second and relax. I remember the picture that came to me of why I had to go down into the cellar. Not the gnome but another creature wished me to come down there and the cat understood this.

Switching on the cellar light, I descend the old stairs. The beast, as I call this creature meets me. Furry and enormous, he could be called quite wild, only he wasn't. He hangs his head.

"What do you need?" I want to say. But words do not come out like that. I kind of choke them out. I recall folk tales of how to tame the beasts. Picturing what nourishment is to a beast, I think of gentleness. Such nourishment feels calming; it comes in the form of a gray mist up the cellar steps, surrounding me. Both the beast and I sigh in relief. I climb up the steps and close the door. He stays behind.

During this week – I decide I will whack away the cobwebs and sit on the steps and commune with it. I had been upset during the weekend. I realized the message of the beast was to give kindness to others, and understand people. I will find a name for this creature.

Gnome is happy to be by the radiator and watch me write.

Have you met the Beast?" I ask.

He stares at me. "We are old friends."

"From ancient times?"

"From ancient times."

"Can you say more?"

"No. You must hear its name. We will go down together, sit on the steps and listen."

"Now it is cold, too cold for speaking. Turn off your light, light the candle, make the room peaceful. I am a house gnome, and I keep the sacred space, and the creatures of the sacred spaces meet you in a home."

Shadows are cast by the candle. Gnome gazes at the flickering flame which wavers with every wind whipping around the house. Fir tree branches scrape against the house.

Opening the cellar door, I peer down to darkness. The cat sits on the top step. Last week one of the hamsters got out and we found it sitting on the cellar step beside the cat. They together looked down into this darkness. The beast crouches on the dirt floor, picking up spiders. It has a heavy sounding name, which hasn't come to me yet. Something like Duddle, or Duffle, or Bubba.

Lately, I started going down to the cellar when I feel upset, and he takes my sadness into his large self and mixes it around with a vapor, swirtls it all around him, and makes these painful feelings vanish. I learned that he wishes peace. He heals aggravations and upsets. Finally, I have named him. He is Bubba.

I don't know if he has been in this home for a long time, or if he has come here from somewhere else. I don't ask him these things. It doesn't seem the time to know.

RosaMitzi, the cat, keeps leading me down the stairs and I stay only a moment, long enough to let go of my own worries of how to get through the winter.

Each winter has no easy way out, but to endure it. Sometimes I ski through the woods, or down slopes, but usually after work, I curl up by the wood stove. I have a book to read. Cabin fever can feel like depression.

This winter, so far, we have little snow. A few inches, maybe 6-8 inches instead of four feet. It has been bitterly cold, far below zero, and single digits by day. Today is the first day in a month to hit 30 degrees fahrenheit. It feels deliciously warm.

My youngest daughter is teaching skiing to children, instead of racing this winter. She misses racing for her school, but she is not in a ski program now. She teaches at the local ski slope, at her high school, and trains with her former coach while attending the local university.

My son is home this winter, and taking courses at the university. He is in need of healing his hip. I tell the cellar

Bubba about my difficulties, and he tells simply listens. He absorbs each problem into his body, and because he can do this, his body is like the consistency of a seal, he is deeply grateful in helping stabilize the household by taking in the difficulty into himself. He doesn't absorb joys, happiness. His role is to calm the storm before it comes into a family.

I walk home from work in the twilight, carefully going through the parking lot of the university. It's a small college, but excellent one, in this tiny town. It is part of the University of Maine system. You meet your profs downtown shopping for sneakers. The parking area is a sheet of ice. Gnome accompanies me.

"What can I think about tonight?"

Gnome says, "Focus on warmth raying out of your heart. Put it out in front of you. Make warmth be around you."

"You feel like this kind of warmth. When you are with me you enliven the space around you."

"We make many places of warmth. Many of us are around you."

"Thank you."

Wrapping the scarf over my cheeks, I feel my breath freeze in my nose and on the outside of my mouth. I pull my large brown wool coat around me. It is below zero in the northern land. O, so cold!

I tell him, "I lived west of here in another part of the north; I had a fur coat. Everyone had them. We got them in second hand stores. We knew they were made from animals, but at least, we 'd only bought them cheaply, and they were keeping us warm." I fumble with these words, not knowing why I speak of old fur coats.

Gnome and Little Gnome are patient. They know I am remembering a place where mountains huddle next to villages, woods are less wild than where I now live, and I struggle with an unfinished memory of time.

I say, "We have a mountain lion, did you know that? It comes around the back of our yard to the compost bin. It leaves its tracks in the snow, going to the pond. Its tracks are very visible after a few inches of fresh snow. One morning I followed its tracks as it wandered from the woods, as if to come to our compost, but changed direction back into the forest. A moose came into our yard, went into our garden shed, then out through its open floor length window. I think it must have been cold. I go out in the early mornings to look at fresh tracks, but I never see yours."

Gnome grins, "No, but I can leave some for you, if you wish..."

We enter the house. I make sure the woodstove has enough wood in it. He settles near me, keeping warm and the cat curls up in the chair beside the stove. I read at a table. The house is quiet.

Wind blows against the windows, the curtains move. I shiver, and wrap a blanket around me. I wish I had an extra layer of fur. Animals have a way to withstand a lengthy stretch of frigid weather. Their fur coats thicken even more densely. They eat more food, especially from our compost pile. In the cliffs behind our house, they burrow into the rock crevices, and sleep close together.

Gnome says, "You could put up tapestries on your walls, like long ago in mansions in Europe. That gives extra warmth for a room."

I think this is a good idea.

He settles on a cushion. "I remember looking on your ancestors' walls in England, with tapestries, and the windows covered in heavy curtains -- dark velvet curtains. On the floors, thick carpets."

It takes a lot to get all this organized. But oil is not going to be cheaper. Wood is expensive--These homes that no one thought about in building them, that heating them in the future would be a struggle. The old timers easily burned 10 cords of wood a winter. If I had the material— tapestries, heavy curtains, I'd sure put them up.

"You will do it, in time, when you have no other recourse, but to make your home air tight. Meanwhile, focus on this other kind of warmth, the heart warmth, remember that," he says.

The winter is no good for a melancholic person, especially talk about how to create warmth. Warmth needs to come from a constant sun, swirling warm seas, a Bahama resort. Alas, not part of my lifestyle. There are the lawyers, doctors who head south during the coldest months of winter here. Going to a fabric shop is far from my daily lifestyle, and I never want to sew heavy curtains for the windows. I stare into the wood fire. I will forget the winter around me. I wonder how to get through one day, let alone a whole week.

"Expand from warmth that you inwardly create, and let it be in the air around you," Gnome says. He shows me how air moves. It expands into many lines. I must put myself out of myself into lightness and follow these lines of air with my eyes, he states.

It has been too cold to do very much walking, skiing. Inside, the dining room is warm, The other rooms are frigid. The answer might be to take down most of the walls, and have one larger open space, that the woodstove would have to heat.

"Large spaces open the heart," says the Gnome. He looks around at the many doors into different rooms. "Not only heat spreads, but also, your eye follows the air lines, inspiring you differently than in small places."

Last week, Gnome told me to observe vertical forces. Put myself in them, rising with them upwards as in a shaft of light from the feet up to the stars. I left off perception of it, about five feet above my head. I felt lifted from coldness.

I put down the book and start to knit, watching Gnome from the corner of my vision. After awhile, I get up to knead the bread I've set by the woodstove to rise. He follows me into the kitchen to observe the next stage of making bread.

Spring 2003

Only four inches of snow remain. We haven't left the Christmas tree sitting on the porch until Easter. We cut up the tree for firewood.

People are saying, whatever can be used for fuel, burn. This includes old clothes, torn paperback books, newspapers. Rumors spread that the price of oil will rise.

The war is going on, in Iraq and our economy is getting terrible; everyone talks about how to be more frugal. The sun shines brightly, but we cannot afford solar panels. To afford alternative energy you must have capital to lay out for it. They want to put huge windmills on top of our mountains, but we won't let the profiteers ruin the mountain ecology.

Maybe it is spring trying to come, and restlessness is hitting me hard. I ignore my gnome friends. They watch me as they sit on chairs, kicking their legs, passing time -- they don't complain. I have been unfair to them, because they love conversations. I have nothing to speak to them about.

Yet, they are still with me. I am surprised by their presence.

Finally, I ask them, do they understand my state, my disharmonious restless urges to flee, to change my career, to change myself, yet I cannot... and do they know I barely see them when I am so tormented?

From a distance, yet close, comes their reply, "Yes, we do."

Then, I wonder, what can I do, how can I get through my day, even today? The weekend comes, and I drop with exhaustion, the feeling of failure so great at work, that I blame myself for my terrible sales, not making enough to make the company want to keep me, I fear. When I keep telling myself that it isn't just me, it is the economy driving sales down, and people's debts up, and there is no chance anyone is going to spend money on a sale from me, I get no respite. The managers say, no. It is our tone of voice. Our lack of drive. Not putting ourselves into our customer's shoes. Yeah, I think, if I am in my customers' shoes, I would jump out of them fast. But I do put myself into their shoes. I hear all about their lives, their day, their problems, which seems to be driven by their inability to solve their debts. Loans way above their heads. I am supposed to loan them money to pay back their more higher interest debts.

Gnome comes close. "Live in the dark night substance of air. Feel it as thick, nourishing substance. It holds you in your form. It can be comforting, peace giving."

I look around at the invisible air. I force my mind to imagine it to have weight, and thickness like mist.

"If you believed in it enough, you would fly, it would support you in a way you don't know," Gnome says.

Well, I'd like to fly. I realize this because I have dreams about flying. It is a glorious feeling, up high, over the yards, houses, hills, mountains.

"Can I try to fly then?" I ask him.

Gnome says, "You can't; you would fall. Yet, in another way, you can come into my world via this air substance. It is in another land, and you must only open a door to it."

I wait, yet he is silent. New snow, called sugar snow, falls. It makes the maple sap run. Fir trees point upward. I gather an armful of wood and stack the woodstove. With some of the children home this winter, the oil furnace burns a lot for heating the second floor. They think nothing about turning up the thermostat. Oil prices are changing. They have risen by 41 cents. When I worry about this, I have to realize how much I like having them around again, hearing about their college courses, and I try to share some of the burdens of my son's pains with his leg. He has to have an operation on his hip.

We hope the war will end soon. Local people we know are there. I am a pacifist, but it makes it hard to speak out about pacificism which I believe in, and not offend these families. We want them home safely. Friends of my son's on his football and baseball teams are over there. When I go to my doctor's office, the receptionist looks worn and anxious. I say to her, how are your sons? She has two over there. She grasps her hands and answers that she prays for them all the time. When I say, I do, too, she thanks me with a worried look in her eyes.

Because we live in a rural state, with low income being the major factor in not continuing education, the lure of the reserves is for this college degree, paid for. My son almost yielded to this. I said, look, do what you must do. You know how I feel, but I am not making you do anything. So, he had the Army recruiting officer come to our home, sit by the woodstove, and talk to him about the advantages of signing up, and then he handed my son the paper to sign up on, and my son paused. He didn't look at me. He was thinking alone. This was before the war, when the world seemed safe enough he thought. Sure, what not? But he had paused, and I saw this. The army officer saw it. We waited. The woodstove cracked, the log on it hissed. The cat sauntered into the room. My son gave the paper back to him, unsigned.

It seemed, until this year, that war was of the past. An old concept. We were technically advanced in warfare not to have to use old methods of the past. We didn't need ground troops. With air strikes, the enemy was found, and defeated. I hated all this talk, but the Gulf War seemed to prove this speed of warfare. In and out, and few casualties. I did not trust this attitude, but also, was glad that people were thinking that mediation, meeting with the enemy, talking to them was the way of diplomacy, not the barbarian methods of killing a human being. What does this prove? What a shock to have this new war arise, and will it create a better situation in the mid-east?

Gnome says, "You are where we are. Play music for us."

I say, "I am way too tired to play music, sorry."

"Sleep then." Gnome says.

One day at work, in between calls, I was looking at a map. I outlined a straight route across country – easy, I said to myself. In a few weeks, my daughter needed to get out west, so I suggested we take this route. We drove out to California where she was to live with her older sister. Gnome started out with us in the car. He watched everything from the window. Landscapes changing, trucks passing. Rest stops where we slept, for we drove almost straight through, stopping off in Colorado for two days. I had stopped to see my mother and father in Massachusetts before we headed off westward. I had almost dragged my mother outside to stand under the pear trees, to be in the beauty of spring with her, fearing it would be the last time I stood in spring with her. (It was). My mother who loved the blossoms, the opening up of nature in spring. She was so frail standing out there, for I had to help her even down the kitchen steps. The effort was a struggle, and I didn't see in her eyes that she understood how precious this moment was to me. She and I standing together for the last time under spring blossoms. Beside her, an old elf stood. We watched the garden plants growing.

The pear blossoms were the most beautiful I had ever seen, and this is the most beautiful memory of my mother under them. The Gnome left me there and returned home to the north woods. He did not fit the landscape of the west. He is lucky he could so quickly get home. I continued westward. I visited an old friend near Santa Cruz, my daughter had a car accident in San Francisco, and my other daughter's first husband acted out of sorts to see me. It was a strange trip.

By the time I finally got back east, I was very ill. I managed to work each day, but dragged myself, much like my mother did to go outdoors with me. I never told her how ill I was, for I feared worry would worsen her state.

Standing with her under the fruit trees seemed like our whole life was in that moment. I would have rather spent a week standing with her under such beauty as spring, than drive out west. Why didn't I? Life is over so quickly, and tears cannot bring loved ones back.

"We are back, look at us," Gnome says.

To the right of me they stand. In the morning, as I awaken, they arrive. After months of being away, they return.

Not their fault -- in becoming ill, I found communication impossible. Not even months after surgery, was I able to make contact. I could simply for a split second sense them, but not make conversation.

It was like looking across a river unable to hear them speak, but still about to see them.

The operation severed me from my body, from the Other Kingdom. Now I know that operations should, at all costs, be avoided, if possible. With me it wasn't possible. I was rushed for an emergency operation. I don't think I would have lived. But then, did I want to live? Yes, I did, at least, there were still things to see to. My children, my husband, family, and many things more. Least of all, I needed to see a closure happen on this job I seemed to hate so much.

I had long weeks of recovery. I didn't have patience with anything other than the effort to get well. Conversations with people with too great an effort. I listened but didn't talk, except at work, which was part of my job, talking on phones.

The Gnome says, "Why not start now? We have much to say."

I rise. Outside snow swirls. Wind are blowing the drifts. Sun shines. The children are away this year. I find this hard -- our empty home. I make breakfast.

My operation left me tired, even months now after it, I come home from work and only sleep. I am gaining weight. I am anti –social. I am fed up speaking to 400 people a day. But I have no other recourse except to continue at my job.

My mother calls me and wishes to see me and feels that I don't see her enough. It is the truth that I don't. Yet now even more than before, I can't. Each weekend I collapse. Driving hours to see her and then when I return, she forgets that I have been with her. I haven't learned to understand this stage of life, where it is only the present that matters. If only I known this then, and I would have risked losing my job to see her -- anything. But now, my body itself is worn out.

Gnome sighs. "Just focus on the surface of things, but penetrate their outer semblance. The chair in front of you, its design, color, use. The cat near to you. The stove, blazing. The house needs this awareness. See the physical objects, acknowledge them in their places. I know there are many things that frustrate you. Don't think of moving things around, or rearranging them. Simply allow them to be part of you in your space. Work on these now, slowly, and see everything in your home as meaningful for you, even a lamp. Observe it, observe everything."

I think of the illness leading up to the operation. I seemed to have no control anymore over my health. I felt like a visible ghost, without a body, because I wasn't present in my surroundings. I had disappeared.

Gnome, I think, in observing people, sees imperfection as a process of becoming perfection, over time. What is not right, needing healing, is his territory. He enters into human conditions. He sees into a person's heart.

Gnomes love liveliness. They help in invisible currents of love. They wish to aid in peace, happiness, acceptance of what is life for each person. There are other beings within a home or forest, who have other tasks. Like the one in our cellar. He sits and absorbs the chaos, storms, upsets.

Light wakens me. Outside, cold wind shakes the treetops, and crows fly looking for composted food. I take longer to rise in the day, because I am very exhausted. I have put on more weight. I feel lead- boned. I am discouraged that the Universal Powers, which I call God, who remains in my mind an elderly gentleman with a white beard, hasn't answered my urgent prayers for help. I am tired of my life. The people I work with are kind, but all of us, everyone in our cubicles, want to move on.

Gnome says, "When you meet someone, hold their presence in front of you. Let them see what you see. Do not be afraid to be the mirror to them. This is your strength, you can help them this way. Don't fear to mirror to them what you see."

I think about sitting in the snack room at work, for the meager five minutes break we get. We think eating a dough nut or peanut butter cracker will make us make better sales. Anything, to get out of our cubicles. So, I stare at people's faces in this snack room at work and listen to the chatter about their children, homes, problems, older kids going off to Iraq, the patriotic talk, I think, if I open my mouth here, I won't have friends. I am quiet. I try to see them without judging their lives. We all gain weight. We worry.

Gnome continues, "In looking at people, don't shift your eyes away. Wait for the sense of meeting them, then, let them, as if a wind blew through, gently drift from you. Enjoy this new grounding in yourself. See them, listen to them, and they will pass on and you can let them go."

I am glad for this simple advice. One doesn't need to get entangled in conversations, but to mostly listen.

Gnome says, "It is the same for anything in your life. If you have a situation where you are confronting someone, or they come to you, ask them in some way why they have come to you, what they need. Then answer it, and no more. This is to keep your strength. Never leave their eyes. Remember the surface. Let other things be. Clarification of intent is the first thing to keep in mind. I am trying to help you regain your social ability with people, but not lose your energy over it."

I ask Gnome, "I find shyness getting worse in me. At my job, especially, it is increasing for me. If I confront people on the street or cafes, I would rather not waste time talking to them, if I think nothing is going to come from it. Why am I being like this right now?"

He says, "Remember the path you have taken, whatever you hold as precious on your life journey, remember this. If you go to work, come home, and have priorities there, like your marriage, then you know that meeting people in town, a confrontation with a manager at work, takes you for a moment from your path.

"It is an abstract painting. Two people meeting, going off their paths, creating an abstraction of energies. Do you see what dynamics are created? How these abstractions move, propel you on? You don't have the energy for them."

Sitting on the sofa, I am looking at the dark sky. Are there stars out there tonight? Will there be snow or clear weather this week? How is it in the most ordinary places the gnome is present for me? Anywhere --at home, at work, he is with me.

He continues. "A secret of life, is to move out of other people's energies as fast as you enter them. Continually move. Relationships of people break up because of new people entering in and creating the abstraction, which is intended to be only momentary in time, as a jolt or single dynamic. Those entering a new relationship can get stuck in it if they do not know to get out swiftly.

"It is not a question of niceness to people. View the situation, treat the surface. Ask the question to the new person in your life: what do you wish of me? Answer to what they need, leave. Go back, return to your life. If an abstraction takes you away -- and it has done, has it not in the past-- you need not dwell on this, but learn from it, and move on."

Gnomes sits at the kitchen table, stuffing now a cookie into a cup of hot tea. He takes a moment to eat it, and then sip the tea. The cat jumps into the chair and sits beside him.

He says, "In shyness, if you wish to overcome it, try to see the person in front of you. Take a deep breath and see each detail of this person, non judgementally. If you seek a person out in confrontation, for advice or a need, you must allow them to 'see' you. This is difficult and you must carefully determine to whom you go. This is a dynamic of life, learning the intent of meetings with anyone. You must learn to keep your power.

Gnome talks about unclear relationships in people. "These," he says, "are very common in your world. It is because of confusion in seeing what is a simple picture in front of you."

"When two people meet and the intention in unclear, difficulties result because the question is not asked what do you need of me?, or honestly answered, and the two often resort to anger, control play, a sexual encounter instead of not answering the intent of the meeting, and this abstraction is confused. There are many broken families out of this lack of clarification of meeting each other. The two people in this abstracted prolonged moment do not find happiness, for a long time together usually because the deeper reason for meeting was never understood."

I must have lowered my eyes, to reflect, thinking that this is for certain. How many times when I was young did I get mixed up with a friend that just wasn't clear. Nothing over the long period of time was happy with such a meeting.

Lights come on in homes down the street. I watch car lights, too, as they pass by my window. The time is not right for clarification with everything, even the long term relationships. Over the years, they can seem to become more and more unclear, too. Maybe, after one's children leave home, intent has to be asked again of oneself and spouse. Otherwise other things fill the gap of not knowing again each other. Is it to explore new ideas inwardly, because one cannot travel easily without money, or is it to give up and sit by the T.V.?

Gnome says, "Be clear with people. Be firm, ask questions. Do you wish to continue in the confusion of another's life and become more drawn more into it? No. So, you see the person in front of you, mirror then every detail of their physical, hold their gaze and address their mind. What is it that both of you want?"

I tell him I want to set firm boundaries, and need to know how.

"By setting your boundaries, you can leave people's space alone. You must reenter your life where you are most grounded. When you are home, you must be present, not with your mind on work. To separate yourself from work can be hard. But where you live is your life -- what you do, read, think, and the family about you, where you are most familiar, even if that life is difficult. Where you wake, eat, return from work, is where you are on earth-- home."

I guess I sigh, for he finds a pillow, puts it on the floor close to the stove and settles down.

He says, "This ability to set boundaries is the key to all things. Do not forget it. Apply it to a manager calling you in to a meeting. Be polite, but create your space; ask a question, what do you wish, why are you calling me in here?"

I think about how a manager had done that to me recently. Out of the blue, called me into her office. Such a confrontation upset me. I was doing well, I thought.

Gnome grins. "Direct confrontation? Well, at least you can avoid some of them. Be direct back, if confronted. Bull to bull. Go around at different angles, never let someone's power get to you. Step back, go to the side, different places around the person. Let the better self in you be listening. Let your lower self, the self that wants to scream, swear, be in constant movement. This is mental movement. Sometimes you can't physically get up out of a chair when a manager hauls you into an office."

Snow falls, dumping two feet. The sky has been gray for several days. Even with this new snow, it is only two months to the first peepers calling in the swamp by the pond. When I describe nature near me, it sounds like I live in the country, not a town. One year, a moose walked the streets. It got too tame. It had to be taken away, to a very wild area, north of us, where he could be safely able to live.

Gnome is waiting for me to recover from illness and surgery. I keep an inside moss garden in a bowl, with a crystal, candle in it. I ask the gnomes for help in recovering my strength. Bending over, doing housework exhausts me. I listen for their words. From far off, I hear them telling me to sleep and rest. That is what I need mostly to do.

The snow is gone, earlier this year. I sit after work reading and usually enjoying my solitude, but today, I feel despair very deeply in me. I am not yet strong as I wish to be. Despair that my life feels so stuck -- sitting in a cubicle.

Gnome has started coming back to me. He asked me yesterday to watch the needles of the fir tree, how they flash in the sun, move with the wind. They move and I sit still, observing their movement.

"This is part of the quickening in you that first must arise then healing.will follow. Move and let your body flow."

They said to be in the fullness of life. To feel the wholeness, the depth of hearts of many things, beating and pulsing with life.

I can't seem meditate for long on these things given to me from the Gnome world. Only in moments, I sink into their advice and feel the underlying essence of all nature, springing into growth. I will try tonight, to put my thoughts into the hearts of all humankind.

There are pockets of snow in the woods. Early, at sunrise, the animals and I went into the woods to sit beside a waterfall. The woods were full of soun, water flowing, bursting water, freed from ice. Birds called. The cats were happy to be back in the woods. It has been a long time.

A healer told me that the best thing on the Spring Equinox is to find a waterfall to sit beside in the early morning. I have done this. Normally, all water is frozen here in the north at this time of year.

Today, the woods are sparkling with frozen crystal drops on dead leaves on the ground. As the sun rose, these crystals lit up everywhere, looking like vast diamonds in a treasure field.

I did not sense the gnomes were with me. It was only I, alone, trying to listen and let my thoughts and spirit be refreshed by the northern woods in early spring.

Inside, at night in my study, I ask the gnome, if there is anything that he wishes me to do.

Gnome says, "Imagine you are in water. Be with the fish within water. Stretch yourself to perceive what they sense. They feel the intricate vibrations of the earth, which come through water and they are wise creatures. Be with them."

Then travel with them. Sit quietly and as you are with them, begin to travel. When you need to mystically travel, enter them. They will help you. When you need to physically travel, be with them . Before you being your journey, swim together, be in their masses, shoals, and then tell them where you wish to go. let them hold the thought for you. See into any pictures that may come to you. Then, prepare your journey as you would anywhere you go. you need to travel but you need to understand how to do so. Do not engage with people too strongly, but let go, and move on.

I visited an elderly friend who spoke about gnomes and how she wished she could see them. She asked me why couldn't she? I didn't share with her my experiences. We were reading about someone else's in Europe, who saw a gnome who lived in an old mill. She talked to this gnome, much as I converse with the one who comes to me. Yet, this elderly person put so much astonishment on this phenonema in Europe, that I felt too shy to say, I have known you for years, I am just very ordinary to you. I don't even think you would believe me, because you think it is so extraordinary to speak with them.

Gnome says "Next time you see her, you must tell her that seeing is in many ways. She knows we exist by a sense in her. But we exist in the hearts of people. If you see us in your heart, this is seeing to us. Seeing us is usually not face to face. Tell her to put us within the warmth space about her and feel our presence."

"This person thinks a lot," I say.

"Thinking has to enter down into the heart, really live in it, not just in laughter or smiles, but forgetting the head. Forgetting oneself. Seeing the person in front of her. Not herself in the person, or her ideas before others. When this happens, the heart has its own eyes, you will see this, if you look into your heart at night. Sparkling little eyes glowing. Then a great change will take place in that person. You begin to be both sad and happy, and no longer sure of anything you believe anymore."

I never saw this friend again. She died before I could get back. She was 103 years old. It saddens me still I couldn't tell her what Gnome said. Gnome shakes his head.

I think of all these things as I walk to work, taking my time. I kick a stone in the pathway, sorry that I take out my impatience on a rock. Birds sing. The day seems to have wings, too. Yet here I am trudging down the hill to work. My cubicle has moved many times since writing this. From one side of the large room to the other.

I pretend that I make better sales calls when I face a certain direction than the other. We think like this at times. Superstition takes the dreariness out of part of the day. If I look to the north, then I can do this. If I face south, then I can do this customer. If I watch the road below the call center, I will see my husband drive by. We stand up to talk, constantly watching out the windows. The managers yell at us to sit down. We try to oblige them but bounce right back up again, out of our seats when they move out of the room.

At work, as I take calls, I scribble drawings on paper. My manager wants to see them, I say no. Why should I show my drawings? They aren't for seeing at work. I store them with my writings about this job each day. I dump them into a box, forgetting them. The next day, I do the same, drawings, then dumping them-- not throwing them away. I have to have a way to go back once in awhile into hell, sort through my box of writing and drawings, shift through the garbage.

At the end of the day Gnome says, "You are trying to heal. Healing is sometimes giving up, like today; take another walk, and this time go downtown, around people, shops, and look at things. Forget yourself. Come back home and work on a project, like a painting."

I want change, but nothing seems to show me where to go, what to do. Everything around me is centuries old. The furniture, the houses, the old roads, forests. Change happened slowly up here in the north. People shop in small stores, mostly, although Wal Mart came outside of town, it didn't dent the downtown economy. People from away ask how did the town do this. I say, well, it is because the downtown business association is a group of very strong, dedicated people who know each other very well, and aren't going to let the town go under. I could go up and down the three main streets of town and name you no business, which closed on account of Wally world.

I wander the streets, and look at pretty things, antique things, modern things, videos to rent, and in windows of bookstores. I go into a cafe and order coffee, sit down and wait for the waitress to bring in. Talk to her awhile, and then read the paper. The waitress was in my college classes awhile ago. What does she do. Well, she is in an art studio cooperative around the corner from the cafe.

I go back up the street, pass the big Victorians, maple trees, and come to ours, which we bought years ago for a song. I am happy again somewhere inside of me. Funny that getting out, talking for a moment to someone, seeing the town shops can lift my spirits until I think of work again next day.

Gnome waits for me on the doorstep. He says, "You don't usually know it, but we have been with you each day at work, and so have many other even smaller gnomes of whom I can't say too much about. They surround you everywhere. They are very interested in what you do at work. You feel hatred for machines. We, gnomes, don't.

"When you start working on your painting this evening, remember that feeling you have. Remember how you feel now after being downtown. Hear it as music, this lifted moment you have had. Try to put this feeling into your work place, participate in the day with a different attitude."

Once I started work on my painting, I felt released from my hatred of my work. I began garden drawings, of flowers. One of them I do when I visit my mother and she watches me, commenting on the colors. I work on this one, and think on her, wishing so much I could see her, despising how I am not able to spontaneously go down six hours south of me to visit.

It is raining hard. I walk to work with an umbrella. The rain blends with my despairing thoughts. Fire seems to rise in me, with such heat that I want to stand out in the cold water, and soak my clothes. Anger wells up for my life. I try to imagine myself with wings, able to fly, able to lift from my sadness. A new stage of my life begins with this fire. I am having hot flashes.

Gnome says, "Experience this rain as nourishment for you. drink in the water, drink and drink water. You love the rain, it feels soothing to you. Observe details of this water as you walk. How it sparkles, runs in ditches, makes puddles. Be in water as much as you can. It helps make the fire go out. When you are angry, put your face into the rain. If there isn't rain, run a sink of water, or take a shower. Adjust to this new part of yourself."

Anger takes me to despair over people around me. I wish for gentlenss, not rough managers barking orders to us. Or other people in my life stomping through loudly in rooms. Even voices bother me. Tone down your voice. Don't you hear how you sound? I wish to say. I am just so very tired.

Gnome sits on a chair in my study. I wait for some peace, until I can tell him about my day. This time a manager has watched me not immediately turn off my computer when he called the team up for a meeting. He yelled at me in front of everyone. Now with me and hot flashes, I yelled right back, and rushed in to the head manager to tell him that I had to be put on another team right away. My anger actually stunned me and everyone. So I broke down weeping at my behavior and then at how I was yelled at. Of course, mostly I was upset I had lost my own cool. I managed to walk home, stumble into the house, go upstairs to the study and rest.

Gnome says, "It is alright. What you have to do is to create a dome, a vault around you and observe it changing. When you are happy, how wide is the space around you. An distressed, how small.

People can mask their real selves, and they don't wish to know themselves, and admit to who they are. When you are confronted by someone like this, step back and speed up the intensity of light around you, circle it around you. Listen, but don't speak. A person who does not know who he is, has yet to find his life. When you step back, you take time away, and enter into a dimension normally not accessed. This is what you must do, and honor yourself. The Universe will help you."

Fall 2004

Sometimes I have taken Gnome with me on trips. Longer ones, like the one out west, he didn't last long on, but left me to return home. But often, he went with me to visit my mother and father. He stood in their yard, looking at the fruit trees in spring, or the flowers in summer, or the great old bee tree in early fall, with so many bees coming in and out of it. I never told anyone about him. He never stayed long, just there for awhile, sensing where I was, and leaving for the north country again where he was at home.

My mother died in November. I walk heavily, bowed in sorrow. Gnome walks with me today. We don't talk, but he follows my thoughts. My mother died with all her family beside her. Before she passed away, I stood beside the lake near her home. This lake is at a top of a hill with higher hills around. Fir trees beside me, and I stood picturing Mother's difficult breathing, two days so far without food or drink and I was in agony watching her suffer. She had requested not to be in a hospital, and had signed a DNR, for she had said, when her time came she wished to go.

As I stared at the lake, trying to understand one's dearest person leaving, one's mother, who brought me into the world, as I watched the lake waters, her young face - a young woman- floated above the hill above the water. The essence of mother hovered there smiling, rejoicing, light-- the smile made me lighter and then I heard a voice as if coming from the hills going into the sky.

"Our princess returns to us." The little people were celebrating, yet at the same time this voice was part of Heaven, the sunset sky, that she was part of the ether, angelic firmament, and I saw a crown descend and be placed on her head. I was sad, the little people were greatly rejoicing. Then I walked home to sit by her bed, and aging that seemed abstract, unreal. I became impatient for her to let go, let her body die and her spirit rise over the lake, the Mother I rememberd from childhood. This person I had never realized was so exquisite. How one takes for granted one's loved ones.

Two months before Mother passed I began to see her as a young woman and I told her this and how beautiful I remember as my mother. She was very happy, as if she would cry. Old age, she had a time with -- she often said that she did not recognize the person in the mirror anymore.

On the Monday before her passing on Wednesday, my father started speaking about the Little People.He said they stood around her bed, watching her. They followed him about the house. He walked sideways often, trying to avoid bumping them. His grandchildren - most of the family had come to be with Mother- thought him very funny, and asked him why he was moving around so strangely. He said there were many little people coming in to see Mother. On Wednesday morning he told us they had left. He was puzzled. Mother died in a few hours.

After her cremation he said they returned to stand around her bed. He said they had been coming into the house for days to help us before Mother's passing.

The gnome is interested in this. He looks at me, as if I need to tell him more. I feel terrible that in my intense inward fight to get well, I have been struggling again with health, that I have neglected the gnomes, yet out of my eyes to the side, I see them, patiently with me.

Be with us, they say. We will speak to you.

My brothers, father and I were gathered for Mother's wake, singing, playing music, and praying. How beautifully peaceful she lay with candles about her. The peace was deep, healing. The Little People gathered were part of the family, it seemed. My father could see them, and made us aware of them. I realized that we see them at different times, for reasons that we don' t know.

I will row the boat and travel with the gnome and go to the city of pink and yellow light walls, and climb the stairs again. This climbing of the stairs gets repetitive, but I do it. I get into a small boat. I row across the sea, to the distant mystical place that I harbor in, anchor my boat, and find my way to the house with the stairs. I climb them, find the desks empty, except for one which is at the back o f the room. Only one person sits at a desk. She looks at me, sighs, and says that she has been waiting. My stories are loing in making I say. She says, tell them. They are part of life, they are part of the living with sadness, imperfection, endless days of sorrow, work, and lack of fresh air.

Gnome and Little Gnome stand around me, at a distance still- ever since my operation. They have let me have a wide space of healing. Healing is taking much longer than what the doctor said. Six weeks he said, but it is almost two years and only now nature forces are returning slowly to me. I tell this to the gnomes for they are distant from me.

Summer 2005

It is midsummer. I am at my father's. The Little People follow my father around. They go on walks with him and are in his house. He speaks gently and respectfully to them, except for the time they were wishing to rearrange the furniture in his room, then he had to firmly say,

"Thank you, I know you are trying only to be helpful, but its going a little too far." He knew from Nana, to treat them courteously, for they wish to help the family.

When he walked into a room, he moved carefully around them, pointing to me where they were standing. I was surprised I couldn't see them as he could. I sensed their warmth. I will always remember how one evening he entered the kitchen and grinned at me, then walked ina wide circle around them. Watch out, he said, we mustn't disturb them.

I sit by the edge of the forest at my house. My home is farther north than where my father lives. I thank the gnome for continuing to be with me. For the many months of being away, that he has had patience. For his caring for the family. I thank all the gnomes for their regard for us.

The gnome is on the border of the forest. He sits in the shade. The wildflowers rise up behind him on the border of yard, gardens and forest. The gnomes love summer, and they stand by RosaMitzi's grave and mourn her loss. I tell them that I am very sorry for her death, that I have been out of touch with many things. RosaMitzi played with them. She spent many summers on this borderland of woods and garden. They loved her. Why did she have to die?

I tell them that death is something that happens with us here in the earth we live in. Yes, RosaMitzi played with you, but she couldn't any longer make it down to the garden, she couldn't walk. She went as far as the first garden, where the herbs grew, and the bushes bloomed, but that was all the farther she got. She was in great pain. Her large eyes stared at me each morning. Surely she does not blame us for setting her free. Her passing was peaceful, as she looked into the eyes of a beautiful young woman attending to her. I felt she was remembering her first owner, whom she loved dearly. At this moment she had great joy as the young woman bent over her to speak to her. She purred with happiness, and then she was gone. I will never forget this purring and then our tears which we shed for RosaMitzi..

Gnome says, "She dances in the air around the garden now. She sits on the steps looking down to the cellar and talks to the cellar Bubba. She wishes you to sense her spirit. She is happy with summer but missing her body. It is more easy to grasp, the physical body, than the spirit. Seeing spirit takes another kind of penetration into a less dense kingdom of spirit.

RosaMitzi wishes you to know she has found your mother. Gnome says I must tell my mother to relax, to view everything around her, the spirit forms of all the kingdoms will then come into view.

I tell the gnome that I am telling my mother this now. She is smiling. She is grateful for RosaMitzi's help. I visualize my mother in a landscape of green fields, flowers, of blue sky and warmth. Night comes when she is sad because she misses us and wonders if we think of her. I keep my mind on her most all the day, telling her things about the earth from which she left.

RosaMitzi lights up in front of me. This is when Spirit is near to one: you have an experience of space lighting up around that person or animal, even a plant. As if one turns on a light in a dark room and a visual image appears. She seems to me a sister spirit who will help me reconnect, and help me onward.

I ask Gnome to help me tell RosaMitzi something. He seems the intermediary for me with her at this moment. I say, "Please tell her I think on her each day and bless her, if that is what I can do. Does she see that we place flowers on her grave? Her grave is near to where you stand at the edge of the forest."

Gnome says, "She does and she understands you. She sees how your operation severed a thread of connection to us. Yet your hope is strong and you will in time return more fully to us."

I tell Gnome, I had a being come to me recently, a strange apparition, and I felt the grounding that I have received from you in these conversations, and I thank you. It was very strange, one that I cannot even talk about, but you will know, so can you please provide safety, and a sense of security to this being, for it belongs to the Kingdom where you come from. Please tell him that he has a home and a place of understanding.

I also say to Gnome, "Thank you for viewing me from afar, and the members of your Kingdom for being with us and with my family. I am searching for someone, who is close to your little People. Please surround this being with safety. Who is this being, I don't know."

It was like this: As I drove through the mountains recently, a limb from a tree fell down, near to me. It almost hit the car. I wasn't afraid, I told Gnome. In fact, I laughed because that limb was for me a piece of music. Music fell out of a tree, didn't hit me, landed, and I heard music. A small magical creature was riding on that branch as it sailed through the air.

I become very tired after our conversations. Tonight, I make a cup of tea, and draw close to the stove, and put on music. Outside the stars sparkle, and I have no sense of season, or time, only essence. I am in a state of simply being.

Tomorrow I have to sit in my cubicle. Tonight, I sit by my stove.

I call out to Gnome. "Hello, I am in deep tiredness, can you hear me? I can't move, can you help me?"

Gnome answers me, "Yes. Go to the woods, to the earth. Feel the wind on your cheeks. Listen to our messengers, be still, accepting. Hear each realm, each kingdom, see them and respond inwardly. Go slowly, walk carefully. Don't look to people now. Search on the little pathways. Our people will surround you and help you."

I go down the path to the stream and the stones. Gnome follows me.

"I walk heavily. Solid, feeling slow, I am weighted down. What has happened?"

He says, "You are in the stones now. You are in their kingdom. The mineral kingdom in the place of the Wise Ones. Absorb the feeling you have when you are in the stones. Breathe deeply into this space. Observe the different stones, and all that they see. It is a place of little movement, the body is placed at rest for the mind to fill. This is where you are now. Don't be frightened. Hear these stones. Stand in the place where you first heard them speak. It is near here, in this stream. Be quiet in this place."

I stay here for a while, and then, I am thinking of something else, and my concentration is lost, and I wander home on the another trail, that other people use, too, and I try to make my body feel less heavy, and will it to move quickly up the hill as I hike back home.

Back home, I lie down again. Gnome is watching. I say, "I am inside, numb almost with that hike. I can't move again. Is this okay? Will you tell me to get up and go outside again, because I still feel like lead weight? It is raining outside."

Gnome sits on the stool by the desk. He wears a wool green jacket and cap to match. His leather boots are carefully polished. They have a rubbed in look of oil.

I say, "I don't want to go out there now, even though I like the rain and wet. What is this state I am in, not able to move?"

Gnome says, "That piece of tree limb that fell near you-- you treat it lightly, but it was meant for you. The little creature is telling you be aware of your energies. Be in your body, in order to understand it. You were driving on a solitary mountain road – alone. You laughed it off, yet, it happened when you were thinking a thought that nearly killed you. The thought went away; the tree limb did not. Do you understand?"

It is true I couldn't remember the thought which seemed to make the branch fall, I recall thinking that, then laughing, yes. Music had popped into my head. Perhaps, that was part of my fear, and music was trying to calm me.

Gnome says, "The piece that fell out of a tree is part of a being, not of our kingdom but another, who wishes to help you. and hears you, and wants to give back to you a part of your heart that got lost awhile back. We won't go into this past. Lost loves of the past cannot be brought back. They drift away into a great lake where they remain for you to think about, but not to mourn. Years can go by before you let them live calmly in this great lake. You will find that in time you can move over the lake water without disturbing the past. For now, when you go to your past, something troubles you, of someone whom you loved, but didn't love you enough to last, isn't that right?"

The past was something that you can return to and wish it had been different. That you had said maybe something at the right time to change a direction that life was taking. An opportunity that was lost, so many things, I thought.

Gnome came close. He smelled of the fir trees. I breathed deeply. He said, "this being wishes to help. You must simply ask the universe for the return of a piece of your heart that the branch falling represented. You must ask for it back. Your health depends on this. But a penalty is placed for you. You let your heart be taken. It has not exactly been stolen. You let circumstances walk into your life, and in full sight you watched them take your heart. You were not acting out of your highest good. The gift of music is part of your heart. You must ask now that time in your life, the people of that time, who held your heart, return it to you. Picture the hidden ones, and part of them revealed to you that day in the mountains. When it returns to you play music for the memory of it in your heart. It will be returned. You will find a time and place to celebrate yourself.

I thought again about the past. It was not only Mabel's death, but other things at this part of my life which had taken my heart from me. They didn't mean to, for I had given myself to them all. Each one I needed to go to and ask for my heart back.

In my mind I went to Mabel and said, I need my heart back, I went to others way back in time to ask for my heart back. I had gathered so many hearts in a basket, then I made them into one large one. And held the basket, but I still to this day, haven't put the big heart, inside mine. How will I do this?

"Can you help me with a crystal?"

I am lying on my bed. I am picturing crystals in my mind. I feel that I can't move.

Gnome squints at my form. "Rest, and picture the crystal around you. Rest in the feelings of this. Take time to feel the rays of crystal energy. Dwell in this place of mineral being where even your hearing changes. Hear the long distances, the echoes, the tones which are like hollowness, yet are fullness in sounding. It is not as your world where souls are close, in front of you. Gradually you will combine the sounds. Hear the crystal tones. Adjust your hearing to the colors of these tones."

I stare at the ceiling as he speaks. I am listening, and finding it very easy to drift off as he talks to me, into pictures of mountains, fields and lakes. I refocus and breathe deeply.

Gnome is speaking, "Become these tones yourself, and feel them as light rays. Your body becomes them. You are outside your body; it has become mineral, like the stones. Step away from your body and see how it sounds and how it changes. Now you can hear what tone you were."

I hardly feel in my body to speak, "It's as if sun is spreading across a meadow. I hear the tones of each crystal sounding, very much as a sea, this incredible sparkling. I feel light ripple. My head is part of this world while my body is elsewhere lifting up into a vast landscape of clear air and white streaming light of crystals. My spirit is free. I can move quickly in this air. My body is the color of sunrise, as if the morning shines on it newly born. I move up and down in the air. Now suddenly a large crystal rises in front of my movement. I must stop. It is hard. I hit it.

Gnome says, "It is bringing you to your body again. Notice how you banged into it. Feel how hard and cool it was, how tall it is. You must return to your body, return to your day which soon becomes night. Play music -- whichever music you like-- but make it yours tonight. Let out this tone and picture the tree from whose porthole a branch and a being as gold came to you.

I say, "My cat just sat down in front of me. She is orange – a golden cat."

Gnome replies, "Yes, she is also asking you to return to your household, but do not forget where you have just been It is real, keep your spirit moving with the crystal light, space, tones.

I say, "Thank you Gnome. The house, and the space in front of me feels claustrophobic, I feel this, but I will go downstairs, and return."

It wasn't long until after this conversation that my job ended. The company told us one day – due to the economy, the jobs are over. They gave us pay to exist for a while. I felt numb, almost as if it couldn't be real. I stood in the bright sunlight, asking the Universe, what next? Am I ready to be in heaven?

July 2005

I am out on the island. I wonder if I can make contact with Gnome and Little Gnome. I feel as if I have stared into spaces that I know are there, but hidden from me, earth places that I had to turn from. It is strange after illness and operation and recovery, I needn't keep returning to this, but my entire body does not feel mine. It is taking me years to feel better. I am not forcing it to be entirely mine again. Something is lost, but feeling healthier is returning and gives me hope that earth energies will fill me.

As I walk the beach, there are few boats out on the water because of the weather coming on. I picture a rowboat coming across the cove and in it, I see the two gnomes making their way to us out the island. I tell them hurry because a lightning storm is coming up. They struggle to the shore, panting out of breath and walk the hill to the cabin.

I tell them to enter and sit down. They relax, shaking off their boots. The rain is coming from the north, a wind blows through the kitchen window. The waves are lapping, at low tide. A sailboat moves into a distant cove to get out of the wind's path. I hope everyone out there is safe from the storm.

The bald eagle flew from his nest towards the harbour not too long ago. I hope he returns safely.

"He will," Gnome says. He listens into my thoughts as I watch out the window to the sea. They are silent, sitting by the fire, looking at me, the cabin, how everything is in its place, ordered. These are ordered lives, not spontaneous, unplanned, scattered lives which lived here in this cabin not too long ago.

The gnomes look up to the rafters, to the books, china on the shelves, the fireplace stones and the old fire screen. "My children used to come here year after year with us," I tell them.

It feels as a tomb here. Memories come here like ghosts. John is no longer here. He'd be always sitting on the rocking chair, listening to the radio. In earlier days he smoked his pipe. He had to give it up because he got cancer, but he defeated it, the doctors said it was a miracle, but John and Janet, his wife, my cousin, said it was the island air which got him better. After the cancer left him he had a number of good years on the island. He stayed as long as he could up here, until the winter came and then they left this summer home for their winter one to return in the spring.

I could tell you so much more, but please make yourself at home here, and curl up to sleep where you wish."

When it is night on the island, and the wind blows, the sea, very close, below the cabin, pounds on the rocks and there in no other sounds besides this crashing, except the crackling fire, pine logs hissing. Tonight the sea sounds like a monster, and the trees sigh and groan as if they suffer with the raging of the elements. In the morning, 'Lord willing' as my mother would say, the crows would be up cawing, and the seagulls crying. Lobster boats puttering around the cove. The sea and water looking as a mirror, with no trace of the rampaging winds, rains of the night.

The next day we spend walking coves and sitting on the beaches, stepping over a little bridge in the woods, to climb a rocky hill to see the view of the next island. Sailboats drift through the water towards the harbor. We read, knit, write. The sun sets a beautiful red across the inlet. The sea goes out to a low tide and rustles the waters.

I ask Gnome a question about my health, which is slowly improving. Why it is taking so long, I have no idea, and have stopped fretting over it. I take each day as it comes.

"How can I make progress getting into this body of mine, feeling I fit inside it?" I have gained alot of weight which I intend to lose, but every time I try to lighten myself, I fall backwards, and nothing seems to lift itself in me.

It is dark. The family is in bed. I am up watching the fire and reading. Gnome sits near me, looking at the flames rising out of the dark logs. He says, "Feel your heart, its beat. Picture it as the sunset you saw tonight, the many colors -- the spreading out across the horizon, coves, inlets. Let love do this, too, ray out, be warm in this spreading out."

The gnomes see my heaviness. "You have identified strongly with the stones," says Gnome.

"Yes, it is granite, not crystals any longer that I am with, " I say.

"It is alright," he says. "The many pounds gained since your operation, are not what you think."

I lift my head. I have been lying on the beach, near to the high tide level where the seaweed, Irish moss, clumps of rope, and broken shells lie. It is the only part of the beach where there is dry sand.

"You have needed to be firm on the ground, to regain your footing. To spread out your being, your inner self, invisibly. You need to come back to the crystal world. This will enliven you and set up movement again in you."

I put my head back down. The gnomes both sit on an old piece of driftwood, next to the purple vetch vines. Sea fleas jump out at them as they shuffle their boots through the dried kelp.

Last year, I came out to the island soon after my operation. I hobbled with a cane up the path to the cabin. Janet was astounded to see me. She had made the long journey inland to the hospital to visit me. I can never forget that. I came up to the cabin hoping to thank her, but she simply shook her head. I had to see you, is what she said to me. I don't know but that she had a similar operation when she was younger. The look on her face as she saw me lean on the cane seemed in total empathy. Janet is like my second mother.

There are people I know I am going to deeply mourn as I write this, only I don't want to think of their passing just yet. When Janet goes it will be the end of my family.

Now, she wasn't here. She had left earlier than usual for her winter abode further south. I thought on her and how her husband and she used to sit with me on this beach. We watched for boats of friends sailing around the cove's corner into the headwaters of the sea. She'd wave and smile, even though they couldn't see her expression, unless using a binoculars, she smiled always to see those she loved. And Janet loved many people. She would be the example of how my heart needs to spread out its warmth-everywhere. The sea, the seals, the gulls, the osprey and eagles -- everything. I would try it-- to let my heart sense the world before my mind.

We leave the island, spending a long weekend on it, having to get back to work. The gnomes leave, too. They get into a little boat, then disappear over the sea. They are home, before we get there.

Gnome says, "We have enjoyed the boat ride, the rocking sea, being in your thoughts, and with you. Look to the winds, make them your sail. Move with the wind as it blows. Smell the wood scents as you leave the island and in the forest at home. Lift as the wind lifts. We can draw closer to you through this."

What we do as we leave the island, is make sure the fire is out in the cabin, the doors and windows shut, then we walk down the hill to the car, go out the long drive to the small tarred road, and go to the ferry. Sometimes we are early for the ferry, other times we have to hurry, and barely make it.

August 2005

A hot summer at home -- inland. Thunderstorms come by each evening and radio and television stations issue warnings. I notice people more on edge, as if anger would erupt at any small thing . I can recall a similar time in the 2001 summer. Then, the air seemed full of static tension. By the end of August I could scarcely stand. I remember walking to the garden and looking at the plants, sensing the air about them, wondering how and why did so much seem invisibly on fire.

In this summer, Gnome stays mostly in the woods. I look up from where I sit under the fruit tree by the garden. He is under the berry bushes.

"Gnome, can I ask your help?"

Gnome has on a green shirt, and suede boots with laces. His trousers are brown. He wears a wide brimmed hat with a long white feather stuck in it.

He comes over to the side of me. He says, "Fire needs water. Always drink lots of water when you feel this kind of electricity about you, in nature. Rest often, seek no quarrels. Seek harmony with yourself. By places of water bathe your feet. Hold your hands in cold water. Touch water often and place your wet hands on your head. Be of healing in your thoughts and rest, rest.

I ask, "What about these storms? What does one do with them?"

Gnome replies," Draw the thunder into you. Did you ever do this? Feel it enter your feet and roll upwards. Feel this as energy and how it increases your vitality."

To work with lightning, like this? I am afraid of it.

"Be well guarded. Yet if you are in need of safety, put the sharp lightening crack into your surrounding space. Pull in your own aura as close as you can to you. Use this also for power, for your personal strength. Never use power over anyone else. You must gain health, strength for your day."

These days I have been feeling very relaxed. I feel blessed that I don't have to go to the job that I had for many years, sitting in a cubicle making calls. Yet, underneath is the tension of what to do next. How to earn a living. I seem to have no goal, except to keep a journal.

Gnome says, "Feel as an open vessel, with air within. It is substance yet you cannot see it. The vessel will fill. But be open to new things coming. Center yourself again through the kingdom of the Little People.

What shall I do this summer?

"You must be in the role you have for your family. You cannot run from this easily. Take breaks, rest, read, garden, enjoy this time, and this space to gain more energy, to go beyond the past and your daily work you disliked. Now you have freedom. Use your time wisely."

--- A year passed ---

November 2006
Changes, new things.

Free from a day job- for a while, that is- I'd been helping my daughter out west with a young grandchild, and we went to France to see my husband's family. I was using up my stipend money from the call center having to dismiss us workers due to financial losses because of 9/11 and the nation's economy which as I've said, we workers noted started way before 9/11.

So, in being very occupied with daily life, I had almost forgotten these gnome conversations. I am sorry. I feel bad about this. I call it real life taking over. Not needing fantasy anymore. Or maybe, my migraines weren't pressuring me so much. I don't know how to explain this seeing of gnomes, otherwise. Early dementia? Hmm.

You see, I had put my journal carefully in a bookcase where I'd get back to it- sometime. Gnome had simply wandered away – like a cat-- watching at a distance as I took care of the children and visited often my father. I seemed to exist only in the present. The stipend from my old job at the call center was running out and so I started to take jobs I'd had long ago, like caregiving for the mentally and physically challenged adults here in town. I loved this job and just why did I leave it? I thought I had to be educated and finish a degree, but then, presto, there was tons of competition for college teaching jobs, and- and. Thus, when my daughter and family came home, east, I looked after their baby – they paid me, and I still cared for the handicapped.

In France it had been 110 degrees but it was dry heat where I could bicycle into the village each day in that incredible heat. Then in England afterwards close to the same temperatures. I was confused about this change in Europe's summers. It has been many years since I had lived over there as a student when summers were cool, never so hot. What' s happening? Do the gnomes have any answers?

I lay down on my bed and closed my eyes. I badly sprained my foot in France, so I rested a lot for months afterwards. I pictured the little boat again, and how I used to get into it, and journey in my mind. I went across the sea to the top of the ocean with the gnome. I saw the sun in front of me as it rose over the horizon.

One day, when I rest under a backyard tree, I remember a recent talk with Gnome.

Here is the climate change conversation.

Gnome had said, "Ask the sun about the weather."

I said, "What is happening to the weather?"

The sun answered, "Heat will change to wind, rain, water."

Gnome had said, "People must make a promise to the sun -- to take in its light and goodness Can you do this?"

I had replied, "It is hard to think of the sun as having personal qualities."

"The earth will only change when this love goes into every heart, then harmony will come. The sun is the secret to overcoming evil. When you work with evil, place the sun around the person or situation. They will feel this, and it will change them. You have to visualize this and let the picture of goodness grow and grow."

Only love will harmonize the weather.

Yes – I had said, Wow. You're joking.

He'd said, no. Not joking.

You have to sit back and be at peace. A cup of tea, some shortbread.

January 2007

I reflect how long it took to be able to communicate with the gnome after illness and operations three years ago. Patience was the only thing I had to go on. I could not force or hurry any connection. Faintly I felt the gnome world watching me.

Then, slowly, communication as in a whisper came back. Lines of energy were shown to me and what kind of energy lines given as a picture each day. Vertical energy, spiral forms, energy circles, spheres, forces were around me constantly. There was little verbal communication, except for what I recorded. They said, see this and I saw the pictures of forms to work and feel part of nearly every day.

To feel part of something, you blend into it, and like dancing a form, you explore its dimensions, but you don't move. You picture the form moving instead. In another life, long ago, I had been a dancer and moved to many choreographed forms. Now, I have to picture the forms in a movement of their own. A circle moves in a round, a vertical line goes up and down. A spherical form has complex movement, whirling up, down and round, and so forth. The point was to be intensely in the experience of their activity. All nature has this movement, particularily in spring when plants are growing.

Again, picture, the gnome had said, a vertical line up and down in front of you, it is an instant movement. How does this make you react? How do you experience it? Trees grow to the vertical impulse. Flowers, people.

Picture, he recently said, a circular form from around you. water moves in circular waves. It is soft, gentle. Now be in a spiraling form -- which is also in water-- It is one thing, then another, up and down circular,

Now, the gnome says, it is time to center down. Think about each detail of yourself, get inside each detail, like you did with nature, years ago when you first began journaling this.

A raindrop, a pool of water. Now be still in yourself. The winter is cold. Although snow is late in coming, it will come. The seasons are changing, they are not the same. Things are later."

It is so -- for in December it was 70 degrees where we have never had this, not in living memory. The snow has not fallen, only rain.

The war in Iraq rages, it worsens rather than lessens international and domestic problems. Although no terrorists have made further attacks, the fear has not lessened, yet we are slowly letting the events of 9/11 recede, not forgetting, but wondering how this could have made the war -- so terrible-- be a necessity to wage in Iraq.

The years of the war make us all sad for we know local people over there with families, children, grandchildren here at home, here in the northern woods. We are always, each day, awaiting news of their safe return home.

March 2007

Snow is deep, sun is strong and gentle winds are in fir trees. It takes time for snow to melt. Often now, I look out to the details of nature and feel close to my mother. Her spirit lives with me as I see the change of season, time and the beauty surrounding me.

Gnome is quiet. He has been telling me again about directions and the way to work within these energy movements. He never repeats the same thing, but makes slight variations of the movement to follow. However, he says he has given me enough for now. Perhaps, I cannot receive more at this time. I have pages and pages to review and work over. As I read through what I have written down, I decide to treat each conversation as a meditation and add my experiences. I have a bad habit of going very fast in indications given to me, like in a conversation, thinking about them quickly, then impatiently striving for the next experience.

It is snowing outside. From my study window I can see the hills. My mother always looked up into hills. She found they gave her great peacefulness. The hills before me are covered in snow. The snow is growing thick as it falls. The north gets impatient with winter, even though everyone knows it can snow here up until May. But we are viewing global warming as a good thing in the north, so why this late snow, we ask, then realize, that the weather is as fickle as we are, and that not even the scientists know too much about it.

"Weather follows emotions," the gnome grins.

"Oh, yeah? I kind of assume that," I answer.

"If everyone for one day, sat in quietness, without fear, fighting, anxiety, war, the weather would feel this. It would take many days of this peace for the weather to change and become harmonious, but someday, people will learn that they and the spirits of the elements and souls within the other world, can work together to tame the weather. If one person were to say a prayer each night for the earth and its elements of fire, wind, water, and continue this each day for a lifetime, this would affect a change."

In Japan they did this with water. Simple meditation beside a lake can help the waters purify, calm heal. Sitting beside a stream and watching the way water drops into coves, rock crevices, eddies, swirls of currents, can heal oneself.

"You must understand that you have a direct relationship, a personal one with everything in nature. A bird that calls in front of you, is speaking to you. Not just to the air. Snow falling in front of your window is for you -- to look at, feel something from it."

I think that I felt exasperation. But snow is beautiful. Uplifting to see. 'Purer than the snow,' is a line from a prayer. I can look at the snow and feel crystals lighten me, if I but take a moment to relax, rest within this moment. Be present, the Buddhists walk their meditations, seeing what is before them, letting it go, seeing again, letting it heal. Gradually the mind breathes again with nature, with the space around one.

What do you hear now?" he asks.

"A crow," I say.

When you heard it, what did you picture?"

"Although I didn't see the crow, I pictured it as black, flying through the snow. Now it lands in front of my window. and looks up at me. Strange."

Don't think strange. Follow the image. The black of night, the black of mystery flying into the white crystals falling. Now take the one picture and create from it. You can do this. A whole world opens to you. Go with the images. Not your thoughts saying that is a crow, dismiss that thought. It means nothing. He gave you one moment of his time, flying down to the ground, landing in the snow, to look up at you."

Yes. I would need to write Sci- Fi, and make a huge story of that one image, but I won;t. Instead, it will remain as a movement of energy for the day. Upward the dark bird flies into the white snow. Upward my soul wings with it into the other world where my mother now dwells. I go to the mystery of creation, of heaven of dimensions, all that we can't see, I go into with the crow. I breathe into this deep night. I slow down, my heart beat slows. My blood pressure drops. I am nourished there. This night is myself, the self of my self that I like; it is invisible and not hardened with the world: illness, or age. Its spirit is adventure, wellness, the journey onward.

"Yes," Gnome says into my thoughts.

"We live on the surface of things, don't we," I say to him.

It makes a short day," he grins.

Little Gnome comes to me.

"Play, play...

Lately I have watched how much he is coming alive beside me. He doesn't seem shy, or holding back as once he did, never uttering a word, well, he still doesn't do that, but never barely moving, except to follow Gnome. He is playful. His eyes twinkle. He wears blue clothing, and a twisted cap. He tumbles, whisks around trees. Is in one place, gone, turning up in another.

I reflect on this. I am taking care of a young grandchild, who also runs, disappears almost too fast, laughs, cries, all in an instant. I am very exhausted each day with this continual play. When Little Gnome starts his antics and acts as my grandchild, I feel so worn out, that I almost groan, o no, two of you. But how delightful and cheerful it is to have children and little gnomes around, I say to myself, but I am not a young mother. I say little gnomes in plural, because always, although this story is about two gnomes, there are many more watching them constantly from the woods.

"Stand as I do, then," says Gnome. I realize that he has always a little gnome in trailing beside him, and he never tires. Gnome is ancient, solid, although little gnome is acting up now, and a handful for him, he keeps his mind calm, and somewhat removed, not aloof, but not engaged with little gnome. He watches.

I think how I have had a continual struggle with my health for ten years. Since the operation several years ago, I am sad often. I long to climb mountains, run, do things I always did as a young woman. Does getting old mean I give up the joy of being able to elicit joy from looking out from a mountain over beauty, land, problems, emotions-- or feel part of the wind as I once used to -- running, always, running. Not even my grown children know this part of me, long ago. The girl who climbed mountains barefoot. Who hiked and lived alone in woods. Where is my soul, I ask of life now.

I have a racing nervous tension within me I cannot stop, and one of my doctors says that it is a virus with a fever. Running a fever. Women at my age walk with continual fevers. Disturbed harmonies of temperature, that identify with weather and its changes completely.

Yet, I am on the way to health. Gnome stands underneath a snowy branch of a fir tree. Sugar snow falls. He watches and waits.

"You must have seen two other ones of my family come visit you recently, no?" He asks me. Today the snow has fallen so thickly that from my window I can't see the hills. Where the crow landed yesterday to look up at me, is deep in new stuff. Wind blows down the lane, and the snow pummels from a fir tree. Birds are warm under branches today.

I say, "Yes, I have seen them. I didn't know what to say about them, though. There are you, little gnome, Bubba in the cellar, whom I rarely mention. He is just always the same and there, and I thank him for being down in the dark cellar. But the others that have most recently come to me-- what must I do now?"

Gnome says," You saw a woman gnome, didn't you, for the first time? Seeing her, took you by surprise, am I right?"

I say, "Yes. You are right."

"What was she doing?"

"She was running, very fast, across the room. I was totally surprised, matter of fact."

He tilts his head. "What else, try to remember."

"She wore a skirt, shirt and had long white hair."

Gnome says, "Then she was checking up where you were, your situation, and little gnomes, and the place you live in..."

I thought about this. He was right. She had glanced around, as she went quickly through the room.

Another gnome visited me, a day before she had arrived, appearing before me, then disappearing. I still need to learn not to stare in surprise at the gnomes. They are such shy people. He had a long white beard to his feet, and was dressed in clothing from two centuries ago: a green velvet suit, white ruffles on his shirt at the collar, cuffs. He had on gold ornaments, but I didn't see exactly where they were placed. Perhaps it was at the cuffs, and buttons. He held himself with a gentle dignity, and I felt I knew him.

"Do you know who he was?" I asked Gnome.

"Did you have a feeling for this?"

I replied that yes, I think he has to do with my mother's forest, and family. It was her line, he came from her side of the family. He had to do with my great great grandfathers' area of the country.

Gnome seemed to agree with me. A lot is left for me to discover. He doesn't want to interfere with my own impressions, and discoveries. If I were wrong, I trust that he would say so.

Gnome watched me. As in a dream, I am left with what to do with the images that have come to me. I can't forget them. Remember what you did with the image of the crow flying through the snowy sky, gnome advises me. Dwell on the image of who comes to you, and don't think hard. Let the pictures come to you of more that surrounds them. Don't worry, you will understand this as you work at it. Don't forget the stories you told your children of the gnome -- it wasn't I, the gnome you told them about, but this gnome is also wishing you to tell those bed time stories, for the woman gnome is connected to these, that is all I can tell you now about her. The 19th century gentleman gnome will help you with his story. Never worry. Look out to the hills as snow covers the trees and blankets the town.

I take a deep breath. Every word I put down has fear surrounding it -- words are hard to describe other worlds with. For now, I will wait and see.

Little Gnome says, "Watch me."

He grins, and leaps into the air, does a forward flip, and lands on his feet.

Gnome stands under a fir tree. He says, "The Little Gnome, will help you with laughter and understanding children."

I had smiled when he said that. I know my serious days far out number my sense of fun. I have always been melancholic of temperament, which means I think but get nowhere. Every situation is worked over in my brain, and I have caution beside me more than action. When I do abandon myself, I am silly, and people laugh, but wonder what happened to me. I want to be sanguine.

Little Gnome wears a long owl's feather in his cap. He wears a red jacket, and brown britches, small leather boots. He looks the typical folk tale gnome of the Brothers Grim, or of Scandinavia. Both he and Gnome seem European to me, more than of the native soil.

Gnome reads my thoughts. He says, "Many people, the visible and invisible are not native to this Soil. Think how long Europeans have been coming to the Americas. Much longer than history relates. Do you think they travelled alone? No, they brought hosts of little people with them, most of them not knowing it. They lived on vessels, and came just like immigrants here. But they stuck to their families in most cases Sometimes a family had gnomes trade places with each other. Especially in a gnome marriage.

Little Gnome is in the yard, somersaulting under the fir trees. A crow calls. He points to it and looks at me.

Sun shines, snow melts. The town is silent. There are no children playing, even cars driving. No one is out there walking. A dog barks.

It reminds me of the day of 9/11 when the town grew quiet. Today, as bright as it is, spring quietly waits in anticipation of blossoming warmth. We, of my house -- we have a house guest- who lives with the family- are discussing on the porch as we sit in odd sorts of chairs, the porch having just been cleared of its woodpile, we are discussing the benefits of getting a masters degree in health care administration. There is an argument going: who wishes to be in administration and not see clients, but earn more, and who wishes to see clients and earn less, or to do both. This is not my realm of experience, so I voice a belief that one could get a degree in one's field of expertise in health care, and be a supervisor, plus see clients... and... I argue that if an additional degree might bring more money to one's family, why not do it? Kind of like, reaching your potential, crunching two years of study into one's head, but doing it. Lazarus arise... have courage, get up.

Our house guest is working on his graduate degree. We sit around the dining room table helping him with things like statistic equations, essays, discussions about the wrongs of the health care system. Then we compare the USA to other countries health care, and the discussions get lengthy. We live in a rural state with many people uninsured. Surely, we think, the USA could follow other countries examples, which provides healthcare to everyone, no exceptions.

Anyway, abundance is not in money. It is in this sunshine today. The sparkling snow. The birds returning, vultures flying high, and this little gnome now merrily turning cartwheels in the muddy drive.

The black cat watches. The orange cat will chase her if she runs off. We have stopped our discussion and sit on the porch as if on a beach and the old, 1950's mail plane, like a loud motor boat, flies overhead.

The crow calls and people's voices drift up the hill. Little gnome looks up. The crow sees the cats. He screeches. He warns them he has his on eye on them.

Yah. I listen to the townspeople slowly awaken as the crow flies off to another fir tree perch.

The other day Gnome was beside me as I walked down the hill to the three streets of town to do some shopping. He plodded slowly along, imitating my slow steps. There was ice and snow along the lanes so I was going carefully. I'd look up occasionally across the valley through the bare trees at the homes and other hill. The homes in winter in this town look like boats in a harbor, so serene, floating on white, eternal snow. These are styles of time: Salt box Capes, Georgians, Victorians. As the town grew, people built according to both their financial ability and the dictates of architecture. The Capes are the most practical homes, beautiful, low ceilinged, and warm inside. I thought of the years of I've been tramping these streets and I am closing my eyes to it all now.

Gnome says, "Sink into the antiquity around you. Don't fight it. Breathe its atmosphere. The peace within form. Except it, inhale the fresh air, this small village town set in the foothills of the mountains. Hidden away, like you. Feel how these old forms surround you, and picture the forest wilderness around you. You will be you.

I walked past little cafes, the newspaper store and quiet lanes. Fir trees and maples line each yard. Some people have tin buckets on these maples tapping them for the maple sap. I look into the shop windows, clothes on sale, always on sale, and a gem store with stones from these mountains at high prices, and I pick one cafe where you can still get a mug of coffee for eighty cents. There are locals talking at tables. Sixties songs play. People have strewn magazines around the window ledge. Gnome has disappeared. I sat thinking of many things. The price of oil rising still, the war going on and on. Young people who sat here, now over there fighting - fighting what? I shiver a bit, and put my hand around the hot china mug of coffee. Everyone is talking these days about global warming. However, here, we have had the longest stretch of sub zero weather on record. We keep our house at 55 degrees always and the woodstove goes constantly.

We sign Al Gore's petitions for the government to make Global Warming a top priority, and make rules for curbing carbon emissions. I watch him smile on television that he got half a million signatures.... we are powerful, the people. I look back at photos of my mother, bless her soul, when she was young, in the early thirties, and at dvd's of the past of Europe as the Nazi's slowly began to wield power. What didn't we know here in this country, taking for granted that isolation would save us, or that isolation was bliss. We didn't know what was happening in Germany. But someone did. Our people, their people were not powerful because we let things go, didn't care beyond the day.

Gnome joins me back on the street. I walk a path to the University campus, just to walk around it. Once I was a student, but it didn't get me anywhere. I walk with this mood of gloom, and Gnome stops me.

"Be in the present," he says, gesturing to the tree limbs and tiny branches shining in ice. Not even the sun's warmth returning deals with thawing the ice up high on these branches. I walk back home on a lane in view of the hills and along low granite walls of the houses. I tramp along, he plodding with me, and that was the extent of this talk, which I had almost forgotten because the little gnome grins in front of me.

As he somersaults and cartwheels in the snow, gnome says, "He needs the experience of communication." Gnome fades into the background. It is almost Easter, and there are two feet of snow. Little gnome seems to be in the air, over spaces, blowing with the mountain wind. Lightness compared to Gnome's solidness and humor in contrast to serious meditation.

A robin lands on the tree in front of me.

"He is telling you to get outside. See how the winds blow today. Little Gnome isn't inside. He needs someone to see him burrow in the snow. Listen to the robins call.

Face the sun as the birds are doing. Look how they sit on the branch twigs, huddling together," he says.

April 2007

Snow is deep. Yesterday I looked out my window at the hill on which townspeople gather to await the dawn. I watched the lights of homes go on, and I knew this year, the first in many years, I wouldn't get up to hear the bagpipes which are played on this hill as the sun arises. Last year I remembered how I went into the woods, without snow, and sat by a waterfall. Not even that possibility exists this year because I didn't want the fuss of getting into snowshoes and making my own trail back there. This year, I watch the dawn from my window.

Small clouds go across the eastern sky. A cloudbank rises above the horizon, yet above this is clear blue sky. Birds fly from my yard to the neighbor's. A wind comes up. Fir trees by the back pond toss. Knowing how cold it is, I don't open the window, but I draw in a deep breath for this loveliness of nature at dawn. Simplistic, serene, the day begins.

Frustration touches me, because I feel guilty I'm not doing something for this day. When I realize I don't want to do anything, I long for the day to pass quickly. I had gone to Good Friday Vigil with a friend. I was deeply moved for it spoke to me of suffering of the world, of our loved ones as they die, of my mother's passing and our vigil with her. The prayers that were spoken for the world seemed my own prayers, of peace, of freedom. Of a time when the earth will be harmonious. A picture of a rose came to me. I smelled its fragrance and breathed in its image.

On this early morning, Gnome answers my thoughts.

"Live fully in each day, particularly on the special days. See the day as a symbol of a great creative process."

I turn from the window seat, and look into the dark room.

He says, " My conversations with you have been this: to be in your body, in your day, moving, living in impressions in each detail, deeply inviting experiences to yourself, because you will grow into them. Enjoy the elements of nature-- the wind -- what it does to your soul, why is wind there for you? Water -- the snow melting. Light in the sky. Fire, in the sun shining. Earth in the grounding you receive when you live into each detail of the day. Be joyful in these things. Joy is creativeness. Sorrow is within your own room, where you are you, if you sorrow. You have to sorrow if you need this force in you. But come out, too. See what I have presented to you in its depth.

"What comes to you in the day, who comes to talk to you. What do they say to you. What do you listen to. Be very open. There are heaven beings, who work with us, of the earth kingdoms. They are not our realm, but of theirs. They and we work together for the good of the world. You will feel heaviness when you are in the processes of the day, but you will be lighter and release physical heaviness.

Little gnome is coming to you for this. He is full of merriment and play. He loves children. I watch you always from the forests."

He bowed to me, and took off his green cap. His eyebrows seemed so thick and his beard stretched long to his waist as he bent over.

I closed my eyes.

I haven't met up with little gnome yet. Injuries to my feet and legs put me in despair for a year, and I work through pain, with an inability to focus long on others. Yet, in the recovery process, the gnome of my mother's forest came to me. He said he wouldn't be able to stay long, but he had a few things to say.

One conversation leads into another one. When you live deeply into one place, you can go many places and find yourself in contact with gnomes and nature.

His eyebrows had thick white hair.

He said, We rest in the stones, because the stones have long stories of the ancient past, as we do . When a gnome says he goes to rest in the stones, he is resting there, for sure. He will take time to be at peace, and not die, but live in the flow of time.

I go out to Mabel's grave and plant the small flowers, which will grow all summer into fall. Along with Mabel, I now think on my mother, and hold them in my thoughts. Mabel had wished to meet my mother. She worried how little I was able to see my mother.

The woman gnome comes before me, looking at me briefly. Hey, I call out -- wait. She glances back, hair streaming out, and runs. Thank you, I whisper. To see you, it is a wonder.

The sky lets down snow. With winter is the hope of spring and that seasons pass and birds return. Spring peepers will call. What is real for me remains around me, plain, simple. Little children following me thru the garden.

If I had known my mother would pass away during the writing down of the Gnome's conversations with me, I might not have spoken so much on Mabel, and, rather, focused on the person so dear to me that most of my life with her I could not find the words to express this. Does one take one's mother for granted, or am I alone in the world to have this desperate sadness with me now -- I think of the many things to still say to her. I picture her in numerous ways, especially in her woods. Trailing behind her, seeing how she looked up into the trees to the top of the sky, there where the trees and clouds met. How her eyes seemed to see beyond the world.

My mother's gnome tells me to dream on these woods of hers. To sit by the stream and hear the water rush by. To see her in these woods, and let this peace come to me. Her love will be with me, even now, it will come from her in the other land.

"I wish I could see where is she now."

"She is beside you, the dead are close by, you know. You must try to see her in a light body, like a new dress she wears. She doesn't have the old dress on anymore."

My father deeply loved her forest. I know that soon, I face his leaving the earth. I cannot yet fathom how he won't be with me anymore. How can I bear his going, too? Like the last walk in the woods. The last time we looked on the water flowing by. My father, laughing, showing us how to make dams in the stream, to find joy everywhere.

Gas beings came to me in a dream recently, and spoke to me about where they could linger. They flickered over my mother's land, behind the cave. They were wondering if the land was a place for them. They were blue like fire flames, but they told me who they were. After the dream I talked to them each day, about the land, that for a century and a half has been with my mother's family and that we children and our children now are the now the stewarts of this land.. I said, "You are welcome to live on it, into its depths of earth crevices, caves."

Peace, I say to them. You are as will of the wisps, darting about, and perhaps you need a bit of grounding: feel free to settle in our family's woods and bury into the forest earth.

My mother holds me in her heart. The fire glows in the stove. Winter is in deep snow. Even higher than when I began this tale. Mabel puts her large arms around us both, big gnome looks on. Little gnome perches on a stool.

She says that life is short, and loving your life is most important. Even you love one moment of the day, sitting by the fire. Your stories will get told. Creatures will sleep tonight.

Spring 2008

My father died on April 10. On that day, his gnome walked into the forest and I sat on the back porch, watching him leave; a friend of mine sat beside me as the gnome went into the woods. We talked about it, as he disappeared in the trees. Sadness and comfort passed through me. The gnome left to grieve, but he will return, and find a family member to live with. I believe that he will go to one of my brothers who works with the land. He will trod the fields with him and bend over his test tubes in his science laboratory.

My father passed from us with peace, joy, acceptance of his time to leave: some of his last words were, "What a beautiful morning!" I will always think of him as such a morning person, up and off, loving the day. I was with him when he took his very last breath. I had to phone my brothers who were taking a hike up a mountain – to come down quickly. He had left us.

Before he died, I told him I was writing down these gnome conversations.

"Oh," he said, "the Little People…good," he nodded. His eyes sparkled.

As I write, the Gnome and Little Gnome begin a jig, and they ask me to pick up my fiddle and join them. Be well, laugh, and try to make someone happy, my father said to me. If you can't be good, be as good as you can be.

"This isn't perfect what I have written about the gnomes," I said to him, "but it is as good as it can be."

"That is fine," he said, in one of our last conversations.

The jig starts up, my Nana smiles and begins her mouth music, and dances. I hear laughter, the day beginning in her home. Tell us about the day, I ask. She puts out her tea leaves into her palm. And stamps them with her fist. My father whistles, takes up his harmonica and my mother smiles.

The family land rustles, and the stream makes music. The river flows on. My mother and father and the little people move on upstream into the thick woods.

Before I leave this story, on the day that Barack Obama got elected as President, Nov 4, 2008, fairies twinkle light in my living room. I blinked to make sure of this. Three fairies were scattering gold dust, which is for good luck. We have to pray for this magic to be with life.

Several years ago a group of fairies about two feet off the kitchen floor, fluttered, and vanished as soon as I saw them. I am not sure what fairies are about, but they are real. Barack seemed to be part of this magic for me. Many people volunteered to help him in his campaign. Is there anyone who can say that …. Nothing is impossible? We called people incessantly to get them out, drove them to vote, pleaded with them to vote for him.

That magic is real. That sparkling dust falls, and lights up the space it vanished into.

So, I have a new day job because the stipend was gone, and other day jobs weren't panning out enough gold for me, so I thought but on reflection I should have just stuck with grandbaby sitting and working as a caregiver. But I didn't. I never take the sensible path.

Thus, here I was back in the same call center building, sitting in the same cubicle I used to sit in. I walk the same streets, and I am feeling depressed again. However, I am not selling the same products, nor dealing with money. A different company, a medical one, bought the building. It is no longer a call center for a bank, the economy went downhill and as did many banks. Instead, it's a call center for medical offices. I now talk to patients all day, who call us in this call center from across the country. I connect them to doctors, nurses, pharmacies.

Some days after work I cry because I feel sorry for myself working here; it is horrid to be in the very same building once more. The rugs are worn, cubicles soiled, ceiling definitely molding no one can doubt that. One of the girls had her asthma act up so badly that her doctor said she could try to sue the company for unhealthy work conditions. That was enough for the company to fear and they got the mold removed. Mostly I weep for the patients I talk to because their stories are so dismal. Other days I cry because I think my story is sad. In walking the same streets to work, I walk with the Little Gnome. Sometimes Gnome accompanies us, but, lately, he has gone to help my father on his journey into the Invisible World. There will be nights when I am tramping home from work, and Gnome is beside me, helping me through the day into night stars. He says to remember: hope glimmers in these northern skies. Or, Gnome will slip into my room, watch me, and then leave.

He recently showed me a white cloud to walk into – surround yourself with this mist – a deep comforting feeling entered me. I have begun to write down my conversations again, sporadically, because another event happened that takes a lot to deal with. My husband has cancer, and this white light Gnome showed me, is stillness, calm.

And --winter is coming.

The Gnomes hold hands with the lady gnome and wood elf, they move in a ring, circling faster and faster, laughing and spinning into the green forest, and spring is happy with their merriment, even if it is winter and I sit by the woodstove. I see them in this mighty vision of the night's dream—it goes on and on. My father and mother join in the laughter and they, too, follow the gnomes and elves. The fairies hang from trees and throw the dust into the air.

Come with us... they call. .. Stars sparkle above the fir trees. Winter snow blows.

Epilogue

Autumn 2014

I started a home bakery doing breads, shortbread, jams and jellies from our gardens. As the bread rises, I play music, believing it gives bread a good baking day. Bread is more than eating it- it is smell, sight, memories, comfort. So are jams and shortbread. I remember my grandmother Nellie as I bake, taste the jam pot after my husband finishes making his famous concoctions. These jams are getting known locally. He is doing better, his cancer hasn't returned.

I call my business 'Beehive Bakery'. We do farmer's markets at this writing. You can see me baking each day at home, or out in orchards and gardens picking fruits. I skirt the edges of forests looking for wilder fruits - fox grapes, autumn berries. I walk up river for these, too.

Big Gnome is now retired, watching everything from a distance. He says he'll wait until the little gnome can converse well and then he will sleep all day in the straw in the barn. It can take some gnomes a hundred years to be able to hold conversations such as you've read in this story.

In the meantime, Little Gnome sits on my kitchen stool. He observes but he plays and tries to make me laugh. I'm a terribly serious person. Big Gnome says I need to empty my mind and that is for a reason. I am surrounded with both grandchildren and customers who have to understand to laugh, don't they? Little Gnome seems to think so.

Made in the USA
San Bernardino, CA
01 December 2018